50 Idaho State Recipes for Home

By: Kelly Johnson

Table of Contents

- Idaho Baked Potatoes
- Potato Leek Soup
- Huckleberry Pancakes
- Idaho Potato Salad
- Roasted Fingerling Potatoes
- Huckleberry Jam
- Idaho Beef Stew
- Sweet Potato Pie
- Classic Idaho Mashed Potatoes
- Potato and Cheddar Croquettes
- Huckleberry Cheesecake
- Baked Idaho Potato Wedges
- Idaho Pork Chops
- Potato and Corn Chowder
- Idaho Potato Soup with Bacon
- Huckleberry Muffins
- Herbed Potato Gratin
- Idaho Style Potato Hash
- Classic Potato and Chive Soup
- Huckleberry Smoothie
- Bacon and Cheddar Potato Skins
- Idaho Trout with Lemon Butter
- Potato and Green Bean Salad
- Huckleberry Barbecue Sauce
- Idaho Beef and Potato Casserole
- Garlic Mashed Potatoes
- Huckleberry Cobbler
- Idaho Chicken and Potato Bake
- Potato and Spinach Frittata
- Huckleberry Ice Cream
- Potato and Sausage Stew
- Baked Sweet Potatoes with Cinnamon
- Idaho Breakfast Burrito
- Huckleberry Vinaigrette
- Potato and Leek Pie
- Idaho Stuffed Potatoes

- Potato and Bacon Soup
- Huckleberry BBQ Ribs
- Idaho Potato Frittata
- Potato and Mushroom Soup
- Huckleberry Oatmeal Cookies
- Idaho Roasted Potatoes with Herbs
- Potato and Kale Salad
- Huckleberry Tart
- Idaho Beef and Potato Stew
- Potato and Cheddar Soup
- Huckleberry Pancake Syrup
- Idaho Chicken Pot Pie
- Sweet Potato and Black Bean Chili
- Huckleberry Smoothie Bowl

Idaho Baked Potatoes

Ingredients:

- 4 large Idaho russet potatoes
- 1 tablespoon olive oil
- 1 teaspoon coarse sea salt or kosher salt
- Optional: Freshly ground black pepper, to taste

Instructions:

1. **Preheat Oven:**
   - Preheat your oven to 425°F (220°C).
2. **Prepare the Potatoes:**
   - Scrub the potatoes under cold running water to remove any dirt. Pat them dry with a towel.
   - Pierce each potato several times with a fork to allow steam to escape during baking.
3. **Season the Potatoes:**
   - Rub each potato with a light coating of olive oil. This will help the skin become crispy.
   - Sprinkle the potatoes evenly with coarse sea salt. You can also add freshly ground black pepper if desired.
4. **Bake the Potatoes:**
   - Place the potatoes directly on the oven rack or on a baking sheet lined with aluminum foil (for easier cleanup).
   - Bake for 45-60 minutes, or until the skins are crispy and the potatoes are tender when pierced with a fork.
5. **Check for Doneness:**
   - To check if the potatoes are done, insert a fork or knife into the center of the potato. It should slide in easily without resistance.
6. **Serve:**
   - Remove the potatoes from the oven and let them cool for a few minutes before serving.
   - Cut a slit down the center of each potato and fluff the insides with a fork.
   - Add your favorite toppings such as butter, sour cream, shredded cheese, chives, bacon bits, or any other preferred toppings.

Tips:

- **For Extra Crispy Skins:** Place the potatoes directly on the oven rack, which allows the heat to circulate evenly around them.
- **Even Baking:** Try to select potatoes of similar size for even cooking.

- **Flavor Variations:** Experiment with different seasonings like garlic powder, paprika, or rosemary for additional flavor.

Enjoy your perfectly baked Idaho potatoes, a versatile and comforting side dish!

Potato Leek Soup

Ingredients:

- **For the Soup:**
    - 3 tablespoons unsalted butter
    - 4 leeks, white and light green parts only, cleaned and sliced
    - 4 large Idaho russet potatoes, peeled and diced
    - 1 medium onion, chopped
    - 3 cloves garlic, minced
    - 4 cups chicken or vegetable broth
    - 1 cup heavy cream (optional for creaminess)
    - 2 tablespoons fresh parsley, chopped (optional for garnish)
    - Salt and freshly ground black pepper, to taste
- **For Garnish (optional):**
    - Extra chopped parsley
    - Crumbled bacon
    - Shredded cheese (e.g., cheddar)
    - A drizzle of olive oil

Instructions:

1. **Prepare the Leeks:**
    - Slice the leeks lengthwise and rinse thoroughly under cold water to remove any grit. Slice them into half-moons.
2. **Cook the Aromatics:**
    - In a large pot, melt the butter over medium heat.
    - Add the sliced leeks, chopped onion, and a pinch of salt. Sauté for about 5-7 minutes, or until the leeks and onions are soft and translucent.
    - Stir in the minced garlic and cook for an additional 1-2 minutes until fragrant.
3. **Cook the Potatoes:**
    - Add the diced potatoes to the pot and stir to combine.
    - Pour in the chicken or vegetable broth. Increase the heat to bring the mixture to a boil.
    - Reduce the heat to low and let it simmer for about 20-25 minutes, or until the potatoes are tender.
4. **Blend the Soup:**
    - Use an immersion blender to carefully blend the soup until smooth and creamy. Alternatively, you can transfer the soup in batches to a blender or food processor. Be cautious of hot splashes.
    - If you prefer a chunkier texture, you can blend only half of the soup and leave the rest as is.
5. **Add Cream (Optional):**

- Stir in the heavy cream if you're using it. Heat the soup gently until warmed through. Adjust the seasoning with salt and freshly ground black pepper.
6. **Serve:**
    - Ladle the soup into bowls and garnish with fresh parsley, crumbled bacon, shredded cheese, or a drizzle of olive oil, if desired.

Tips:

- **For Extra Flavor:** Add a splash of white wine or a pinch of thyme during the cooking process.
- **For a Vegetarian Version:** Use vegetable broth and skip the bacon garnish.
- **For Creamier Soup:** Use a higher ratio of heavy cream or substitute with half-and-half.

Enjoy your hearty and comforting Potato Leek Soup, perfect for warming up on a chilly day!

Huckleberry Pancakes

Ingredients:

- **For the Pancakes:**
    - 1 cup all-purpose flour
    - 2 tablespoons granulated sugar
    - 1 tablespoon baking powder
    - 1/2 teaspoon salt
    - 1 cup milk (whole or 2%)
    - 1 large egg
    - 2 tablespoons unsalted butter, melted
    - 1 teaspoon vanilla extract
    - 1 cup fresh or frozen huckleberries (if using frozen, do not thaw)
- **For Serving (optional):**
    - Maple syrup
    - Whipped cream
    - Additional huckleberries
    - Powdered sugar

Instructions:

1. **Prepare the Dry Ingredients:**
    - In a large bowl, whisk together the flour, sugar, baking powder, and salt.
2. **Prepare the Wet Ingredients:**
    - In a separate bowl, mix together the milk, egg, melted butter, and vanilla extract.
3. **Combine the Ingredients:**
    - Pour the wet ingredients into the dry ingredients and stir gently until just combined. The batter will be a bit lumpy; do not overmix.
    - Fold in the huckleberries gently, being careful not to break them up too much.
4. **Cook the Pancakes:**
    - Heat a griddle or non-stick skillet over medium heat. Lightly grease with butter or oil.
    - Pour 1/4 cup of batter onto the hot griddle for each pancake. Use the back of a spoon to spread the batter into a round shape if needed.
    - Cook until bubbles form on the surface of the pancake and the edges look set, about 2-3 minutes.
    - Flip the pancake and cook for an additional 1-2 minutes, or until golden brown and cooked through.
    - Keep the pancakes warm in a low oven while you cook the remaining pancakes.
5. **Serve:**
    - Stack the pancakes on a plate and serve with maple syrup, whipped cream, and additional huckleberries if desired.
    - Dust with powdered sugar for a touch of sweetness.

Tips:

- **For Fluffier Pancakes:** Allow the batter to rest for about 5 minutes before cooking. This helps the baking powder work better and results in fluffier pancakes.
- **For Even Cooking:** Make sure your griddle or skillet is preheated and evenly heated to avoid unevenly cooked pancakes.
- **For a Delicious Twist:** Add a sprinkle of lemon zest or a touch of cinnamon to the batter for extra flavor.

Enjoy your Huckleberry Pancakes, a wonderful treat that captures the essence of the wild and sweet huckleberry!

Idaho Potato Salad

Ingredients:

- **For the Salad:**
    - 4 large Idaho russet potatoes, peeled and diced
    - 4 large eggs
    - 1 cup celery, finely chopped
    - 1/2 cup red onion, finely chopped
    - 1/2 cup sweet pickles or pickle relish
    - 1/4 cup fresh parsley, chopped
- **For the Dressing:**
    - 1 cup mayonnaise
    - 2 tablespoons Dijon mustard
    - 1 tablespoon apple cider vinegar
    - 1 tablespoon fresh lemon juice
    - Salt and freshly ground black pepper, to taste

Instructions:

1. **Cook the Potatoes and Eggs:**
    - Place the diced potatoes in a large pot and cover with cold water. Add a pinch of salt.
    - Bring to a boil over medium-high heat, then reduce the heat and simmer for 10-12 minutes, or until the potatoes are tender but still firm.
    - While the potatoes are cooking, place the eggs in a separate pot and cover with cold water. Bring to a boil, then remove from heat and let sit for 10-12 minutes. Drain and cool the eggs under cold running water. Peel and chop them.
2. **Prepare the Ingredients:**
    - Drain the cooked potatoes and let them cool slightly.
    - In a large bowl, combine the chopped eggs, celery, red onion, sweet pickles or relish, and fresh parsley.
3. **Make the Dressing:**
    - In a small bowl, whisk together the mayonnaise, Dijon mustard, apple cider vinegar, and lemon juice. Season with salt and freshly ground black pepper to taste.
4. **Combine the Salad:**
    - Add the cooled potatoes to the bowl with the other ingredients.
    - Pour the dressing over the mixture and gently fold until everything is well combined and coated with the dressing.
5. **Chill and Serve:**
    - Cover the potato salad with plastic wrap and refrigerate for at least 1 hour before serving to allow the flavors to meld.
    - Adjust seasoning with additional salt and pepper if needed before serving.

Tips:

- **For Extra Flavor:** Add a tablespoon of chopped fresh dill or chives to the salad for an extra burst of flavor.
- **For Creamier Texture:** You can add a little bit of sour cream or Greek yogurt to the dressing for added creaminess and tang.
- **For a Twist:** Incorporate some cooked bacon bits or a handful of chopped green onions for added texture and flavor.

Enjoy your Idaho Potato Salad, a classic and satisfying side dish that highlights the rich, creamy taste of Idaho russet potatoes!

Roasted Fingerling Potatoes

Ingredients:

- 1 pound fingerling potatoes
- 2 tablespoons olive oil
- 1 teaspoon fresh rosemary or thyme, chopped (or 1/2 teaspoon dried)
- 3 cloves garlic, minced
- Salt and freshly ground black pepper, to taste
- Optional: 1 tablespoon balsamic vinegar or lemon juice for extra flavor

Instructions:

1. **Preheat Oven:**
   - Preheat your oven to 400°F (200°C).
2. **Prepare the Potatoes:**
   - Wash and scrub the fingerling potatoes thoroughly. Pat them dry with a towel.
   - Depending on their size, you may want to cut larger potatoes in half lengthwise to ensure even cooking.
3. **Season the Potatoes:**
   - In a large bowl, toss the fingerling potatoes with olive oil, minced garlic, chopped rosemary or thyme, salt, and freshly ground black pepper.
   - If using balsamic vinegar or lemon juice, add it to the bowl and toss to coat the potatoes evenly.
4. **Roast the Potatoes:**
   - Spread the seasoned potatoes in a single layer on a baking sheet. Make sure the potatoes are not overcrowded to allow for even roasting.
   - Roast in the preheated oven for 25-30 minutes, or until the potatoes are golden brown and tender when pierced with a fork. Halfway through roasting, toss the potatoes to ensure even browning.
5. **Serve:**
   - Remove the potatoes from the oven and let them cool slightly before serving.
   - Garnish with additional fresh herbs if desired, and serve warm.

Tips:

- **For Extra Crispiness:** Use a high-quality olive oil and make sure the potatoes are spread out in a single layer on the baking sheet.
- **For Added Flavor:** You can also sprinkle some grated Parmesan cheese over the potatoes during the last 5 minutes of roasting for a cheesy, crispy topping.
- **For a Different Twist:** Try adding other seasonings like smoked paprika, cumin, or even a pinch of chili flakes for a bit of heat.

Enjoy your Roasted Fingerling Potatoes, a delicious and versatile side dish that's sure to be a hit at your next meal!

Huckleberry Jam

Ingredients:

- 4 cups fresh or frozen huckleberries (thawed if frozen)
- 1/4 cup lemon juice (freshly squeezed)
- 1/4 cup water
- 1 package (1.75 oz) fruit pectin (like Sure-Jell)
- 5 cups granulated sugar
- 1/2 teaspoon butter (optional, to reduce foaming)

Instructions:

1. **Prepare the Jars:**
    - Sterilize your canning jars and lids by placing them in a boiling water bath for 10 minutes. Keep them hot until ready to use.
2. **Cook the Huckleberries:**
    - In a large saucepan, combine the huckleberries, lemon juice, and water.
    - Bring the mixture to a boil over medium heat, stirring occasionally.
3. **Add the Pectin:**
    - Stir in the fruit pectin. Continue to cook the mixture, stirring constantly, until it comes to a full rolling boil (a boil that cannot be stirred down).
4. **Add the Sugar:**
    - Once the mixture reaches a rolling boil, add the granulated sugar all at once. Stir until the sugar is completely dissolved and the mixture returns to a boil.
    - Boil the mixture for 1-2 minutes, or until it reaches the gel stage. You can check the gel stage by placing a spoonful of the hot jam on a cold plate and running your finger through it. If it wrinkles and holds its shape, it's ready. If not, continue boiling for another minute and test again.
5. **Skim the Foam:**
    - If there is any foam on the surface of the jam, you can skim it off with a spoon. Adding a small amount of butter (1/2 teaspoon) can help reduce foaming.
6. **Fill the Jars:**
    - Pour the hot jam into the prepared sterilized jars, leaving about 1/4-inch headspace at the top. Wipe the rims of the jars with a clean, damp cloth to remove any residue.
7. **Seal the Jars:**
    - Place the sterilized lids on the jars and screw on the metal bands until they are fingertip-tight.
8. **Process the Jars:**
    - Process the jars in a boiling water bath for 5-10 minutes to ensure they are sealed properly. The water should cover the jars by at least 1 inch.
    - Remove the jars from the water bath and let them cool on a clean towel or rack. You should hear a popping sound as the jars seal.

9. **Check the Seals:**
   - Once the jars are completely cool, check the seals by pressing down in the center of each lid. If it does not pop back, the jar has sealed properly. If it does pop, refrigerate the jar and use it within a few weeks.

Tips:

- **For Consistent Results:** Make sure to measure ingredients accurately and follow the recipe closely.
- **To Test Jam Readiness:** If you have a candy thermometer, the jam should reach 220°F (104°C) for proper consistency.
- **Storage:** Store sealed jars in a cool, dark place. Properly sealed, homemade jam can last up to a year.

Enjoy your homemade Huckleberry Jam spread on toast, mixed into yogurt, or as a topping for desserts!

Idaho Beef Stew

Ingredients:

- **For the Stew:**
    - 2 pounds beef chuck, cut into 1-inch cubes
    - 2 tablespoons vegetable oil
    - 1 large onion, chopped
    - 3 cloves garlic, minced
    - 4 large Idaho russet potatoes, peeled and cut into chunks
    - 4 carrots, peeled and sliced
    - 2 celery stalks, sliced
    - 1 cup green peas (fresh or frozen)
    - 1 cup red wine (optional, or use extra beef broth)
    - 4 cups beef broth
    - 1 can (14.5 oz) diced tomatoes, with juice
    - 2 tablespoons tomato paste
    - 1 tablespoon Worcestershire sauce
    - 2 teaspoons dried thyme
    - 1 teaspoon dried rosemary
    - 2 bay leaves
    - Salt and freshly ground black pepper, to taste
    - 2 tablespoons all-purpose flour (optional, for thickening)
- **For Garnish (optional):**
    - Fresh parsley, chopped

Instructions:

1. **Brown the Beef:**
    - In a large pot or Dutch oven, heat the vegetable oil over medium-high heat.
    - Add the beef cubes in batches, making sure not to overcrowd the pot. Brown the beef on all sides. Remove the beef with a slotted spoon and set aside.
2. **Sauté the Aromatics:**
    - In the same pot, add the chopped onion and cook for about 5 minutes, or until softened.
    - Add the minced garlic and cook for an additional 1-2 minutes until fragrant.
3. **Deglaze the Pot:**
    - If using red wine, pour it into the pot and scrape up any browned bits from the bottom with a wooden spoon. Let the wine reduce for 2-3 minutes. If not using wine, skip this step.
4. **Combine Ingredients:**
    - Return the browned beef to the pot. Add the beef broth, diced tomatoes with juice, tomato paste, Worcestershire sauce, thyme, rosemary, and bay leaves. Stir to combine.

     - Bring the mixture to a boil, then reduce the heat to low.
5. **Simmer the Stew:**
     - Cover the pot and let it simmer for 1 to 1.5 hours, or until the beef is tender.
6. **Add Vegetables:**
     - Add the potatoes, carrots, and celery to the pot. Continue to simmer, covered, for another 30-40 minutes, or until the vegetables are tender.
7. **Thicken the Stew (Optional):**
     - If you prefer a thicker stew, mix 2 tablespoons of flour with a small amount of water to create a slurry. Stir the slurry into the stew and cook for an additional 5-10 minutes until thickened.
8. **Add Peas and Final Seasoning:**
     - Stir in the green peas and cook for an additional 5 minutes.
     - Remove the bay leaves and adjust seasoning with salt and freshly ground black pepper to taste.
9. **Serve:**
     - Ladle the stew into bowls and garnish with chopped fresh parsley if desired.

Tips:

- **For Extra Flavor:** Consider adding a splash of balsamic vinegar or a teaspoon of soy sauce to deepen the flavor.
- **For a Richer Stew:** You can use beef broth made from beef bones for a richer taste.
- **Storage:** Store leftovers in an airtight container in the refrigerator for up to 3-4 days, or freeze for up to 3 months.

Enjoy your hearty and flavorful Idaho Beef Stew, perfect for a comforting meal!

Sweet Potato Pie

Ingredients:

- **For the Pie Crust:**
    - 1 1/2 cups all-purpose flour
    - 1/4 teaspoon salt
    - 1/2 cup unsalted butter, cold and cut into small pieces
    - 1/4 cup granulated sugar (optional)
    - 3-4 tablespoons ice water
- **For the Sweet Potato Filling:**
    - 2 cups cooked and mashed sweet potatoes (about 2 medium sweet potatoes)
    - 1 cup granulated sugar
    - 1/2 cup packed brown sugar
    - 1/2 cup evaporated milk
    - 2 large eggs
    - 1/2 cup melted unsalted butter
    - 1 teaspoon vanilla extract
    - 1 teaspoon ground cinnamon
    - 1/2 teaspoon ground nutmeg
    - 1/4 teaspoon ground allspice
    - 1/4 teaspoon ground ginger
    - Pinch of salt

Instructions:

1. **Prepare the Pie Crust:**
    - In a large bowl, whisk together the flour and salt.
    - Cut in the cold butter using a pastry blender or your fingers until the mixture resembles coarse crumbs.
    - If using sugar, mix it in with the flour and butter.
    - Gradually add ice water, 1 tablespoon at a time, until the dough begins to come together. You may not need all the water.
    - Gather the dough into a ball, flatten it into a disk, wrap it in plastic wrap, and refrigerate for at least 30 minutes.
2. **Preheat the Oven:**
    - Preheat your oven to 375°F (190°C).
3. **Prepare the Filling:**
    - In a large bowl, combine the mashed sweet potatoes, granulated sugar, brown sugar, evaporated milk, eggs, melted butter, vanilla extract, cinnamon, nutmeg, allspice, ginger, and salt. Mix until smooth and well combined.
4. **Roll Out the Pie Crust:**
    - On a lightly floured surface, roll out the chilled dough to fit a 9-inch pie dish. Transfer the dough to the pie dish, trimming any excess and crimping the edges.

- If desired, you can also blind-bake the crust for a few minutes to prevent it from becoming soggy. To do this, line the crust with parchment paper and fill with pie weights or dried beans. Bake for 10 minutes, then remove the weights and paper and bake for an additional 5 minutes.
5. **Fill and Bake the Pie:**
    - Pour the sweet potato filling into the prepared pie crust, spreading it evenly.
    - Bake in the preheated oven for 50-60 minutes, or until the filling is set and the edges of the crust are golden brown. A knife inserted into the center should come out clean.
6. **Cool and Serve:**
    - Allow the pie to cool completely on a wire rack before slicing. This helps the filling to set properly.
7. **Serve:**
    - Serve the pie as is, or with a dollop of whipped cream or a scoop of vanilla ice cream if desired.

Tips:

- **For Creamier Filling:** Use fresh sweet potatoes that are well-cooked and thoroughly mashed. Avoid any lumps in the filling.
- **For a Flakier Crust:** Ensure your butter is very cold when cutting it into the flour, and avoid overworking the dough.
- **Make Ahead:** The pie can be made ahead of time and stored in the refrigerator for up to 3 days, or frozen for up to 2 months. If freezing, wrap it tightly in plastic wrap and foil.

Enjoy your delicious Sweet Potato Pie, a classic and comforting dessert that's perfect for any occasion!

Classic Idaho Mashed Potatoes

Ingredients:

- 2 pounds Idaho russet potatoes (about 4 large potatoes)
- 1/2 cup whole milk (or heavy cream for extra richness)
- 1/4 cup unsalted butter, cut into small pieces
- Salt and freshly ground black pepper, to taste
- Optional: 1/4 cup sour cream or cream cheese for extra creaminess
- Optional: Fresh chives or parsley, chopped, for garnish

Instructions:

1. **Prepare the Potatoes:**
   - Peel the potatoes and cut them into even-sized chunks (about 1-2 inches each). This ensures they cook evenly.
2. **Cook the Potatoes:**
   - Place the potato chunks in a large pot and cover with cold water by about 1 inch. Add a generous pinch of salt to the water.
   - Bring the water to a boil over medium-high heat, then reduce the heat and let the potatoes simmer for 15-20 minutes, or until they are tender and easily pierced with a fork.
3. **Drain and Dry:**
   - Drain the potatoes well in a colander. Let them sit for a few minutes to allow excess moisture to evaporate.
4. **Mash the Potatoes:**
   - Return the drained potatoes to the pot or a large bowl. Use a potato masher to begin mashing the potatoes. For a smoother texture, you can use a potato ricer or food mill.
5. **Add Milk and Butter:**
   - Gradually add the milk and butter to the mashed potatoes, mixing until smooth and creamy. If you prefer extra creamy mashed potatoes, you can also mix in sour cream or cream cheese.
6. **Season:**
   - Season the mashed potatoes with salt and freshly ground black pepper to taste. Stir until well combined.
7. **Optional Garnish:**
   - If desired, garnish the mashed potatoes with chopped fresh chives or parsley for added color and flavor.
8. **Serve:**
   - Serve the mashed potatoes hot, as a side dish with your favorite main courses.

Tips:

- **For Creamier Potatoes:** Use warm milk and melted butter to prevent cooling down the potatoes and to help them absorb the liquids better.
- **For Fluffier Potatoes:** Avoid over-mashing, as this can make the potatoes gummy. If you prefer a very smooth texture, use a potato ricer or food mill.
- **Make Ahead:** Mashed potatoes can be made ahead of time and kept warm in a slow cooker on the "keep warm" setting for several hours. You can also reheat them in the microwave or on the stove, adding a bit more milk if needed.

Enjoy your classic Idaho Mashed Potatoes, a comforting and versatile side dish that pairs perfectly with a variety of meals!

Potato and Cheddar Croquettes

Ingredients:

- **For the Croquettes:**
    - 2 cups leftover mashed potatoes (or freshly made mashed potatoes)
    - 1 cup shredded sharp cheddar cheese
    - 1/4 cup finely chopped fresh chives or parsley
    - 1/4 teaspoon garlic powder
    - 1/4 teaspoon onion powder
    - Salt and freshly ground black pepper, to taste
    - 1/2 cup all-purpose flour
    - 2 large eggs, beaten
    - 1 cup breadcrumbs (preferably panko for extra crispiness)
    - Vegetable oil, for frying
- **For Serving (optional):**
    - Sour cream or ranch dressing
    - Additional chopped chives or parsley

Instructions:

1. **Prepare the Mixture:**
    - In a large bowl, combine the mashed potatoes, shredded cheddar cheese, chopped chives or parsley, garlic powder, onion powder, salt, and pepper. Mix until well combined.
2. **Form the Croquettes:**
    - Shape the potato mixture into small balls or oval shapes, about 1-2 inches in diameter, and set them on a baking sheet or plate.
3. **Coat the Croquettes:**
    - Set up a breading station: Place the flour in one shallow dish, the beaten eggs in another, and the breadcrumbs in a third dish.
    - Roll each potato ball first in the flour, then dip it in the beaten eggs, and finally coat it with breadcrumbs, pressing gently to adhere.
4. **Fry the Croquettes:**
    - Heat about 1/2 inch of vegetable oil in a large skillet over medium heat. Test the oil by dropping a small breadcrumb into it; if it sizzles, the oil is ready.
    - Fry the croquettes in batches, making sure not to overcrowd the pan. Cook for about 2-3 minutes per side, or until golden brown and crispy.
    - Remove the croquettes from the skillet and drain them on a plate lined with paper towels.
5. **Serve:**
    - Serve the potato and cheddar croquettes warm with a side of sour cream or ranch dressing if desired.
    - Garnish with additional chopped chives or parsley for extra color and flavor.

Tips:

- **For Even Cooking:** Ensure the oil is hot enough before adding the croquettes to prevent them from becoming greasy. Maintain the oil temperature between 350°F (175°C) and 375°F (190°C).
- **For Baking Option:** If you prefer to bake the croquettes, place them on a baking sheet lined with parchment paper, spray lightly with cooking oil, and bake in a preheated oven at 400°F (200°C) for about 20-25 minutes, turning halfway through, until golden and crispy.
- **Make Ahead:** You can prepare the croquettes in advance and freeze them before frying. Place them on a baking sheet in a single layer, freeze until firm, then transfer to a freezer bag. Fry from frozen, adding a couple of extra minutes to the cooking time.

Enjoy your crispy, cheesy Potato and Cheddar Croquettes, perfect for a snack, appetizer, or side dish!

Huckleberry Cheesecake

Ingredients:

- **For the Crust:**
    - 1 1/2 cups graham cracker crumbs (about 12 whole graham crackers, crushed)
    - 1/4 cup granulated sugar
    - 1/2 cup unsalted butter, melted
- **For the Huckleberry Swirl:**
    - 1 cup huckleberries (fresh or frozen, thawed if frozen)
    - 1/4 cup granulated sugar
    - 1 tablespoon lemon juice
    - 1 tablespoon water (if needed)
- **For the Cheesecake Filling:**
    - 4 (8 oz) packages cream cheese, softened
    - 1 cup granulated sugar
    - 1 teaspoon vanilla extract
    - 4 large eggs
    - 1 cup sour cream
    - 1 cup heavy cream

Instructions:

1. **Preheat Oven:**
    - Preheat your oven to 325°F (163°C).
2. **Prepare the Crust:**
    - In a medium bowl, mix together the graham cracker crumbs, granulated sugar, and melted butter until the mixture resembles wet sand.
    - Press the mixture evenly into the bottom of a 9-inch springform pan. Use the back of a spoon to pack it down firmly.
    - Bake the crust in the preheated oven for 10 minutes. Remove from the oven and let it cool while you prepare the filling.
3. **Prepare the Huckleberry Swirl:**
    - In a small saucepan, combine the huckleberries, granulated sugar, and lemon juice. Cook over medium heat until the berries break down and the mixture thickens slightly, about 5-7 minutes. If the mixture is too thick, add a tablespoon of water.
    - Let the huckleberry mixture cool to room temperature.
4. **Prepare the Cheesecake Filling:**
    - In a large bowl, beat the softened cream cheese with an electric mixer until smooth and creamy.
    - Gradually add the granulated sugar and vanilla extract, beating until combined.
    - Add the eggs one at a time, beating well after each addition.
    - Mix in the sour cream and heavy cream until the batter is smooth.

5. **Assemble the Cheesecake:**
   - Pour the cheesecake filling over the cooled crust in the springform pan.
   - Drop spoonfuls of the huckleberry mixture over the top of the cheesecake batter.
   - Use a knife or a toothpick to swirl the huckleberry mixture into the cheesecake filling, creating a marbled effect.
6. **Bake the Cheesecake:**
   - Place the springform pan on a baking sheet to catch any drips. Bake the cheesecake in the preheated oven for 60-70 minutes, or until the center is set but still slightly jiggly.
   - Turn off the oven and crack the oven door slightly. Let the cheesecake cool in the oven for 1 hour to prevent cracking.
7. **Chill and Serve:**
   - Remove the cheesecake from the oven and refrigerate it for at least 4 hours or overnight to fully set.
   - Before serving, remove the cheesecake from the springform pan and transfer it to a serving plate.

Tips:

- **Prevent Cracking:** Bake the cheesecake in a water bath (place the springform pan inside a larger baking pan filled with hot water) to help regulate the temperature and reduce the risk of cracking.
- **Smooth Filling:** Ensure all ingredients for the filling are at room temperature to prevent lumps.
- **Decorate:** You can top the cheesecake with additional huckleberries or a huckleberry sauce before serving for extra flair.

Enjoy your rich and creamy Huckleberry Cheesecake, a delightful dessert that's sure to impress!

Baked Idaho Potato Wedges

Ingredients:

- 4 large Idaho russet potatoes
- 2-3 tablespoons olive oil
- 1 teaspoon garlic powder
- 1 teaspoon onion powder
- 1 teaspoon paprika
- 1/2 teaspoon dried oregano or rosemary (optional)
- Salt and freshly ground black pepper, to taste
- Optional: 1/4 cup grated Parmesan cheese
- Optional: Fresh parsley or chives, chopped, for garnish

Instructions:

1. **Preheat Oven:**
    - Preheat your oven to 425°F (220°C). Line a large baking sheet with parchment paper or lightly grease it.
2. **Prepare the Potatoes:**
    - Wash and scrub the potatoes. You can peel them if you prefer, but keeping the skin on adds extra texture and flavor.
    - Cut each potato in half lengthwise, then cut each half into 4-6 wedges, depending on the size of the potato.
3. **Season the Potatoes:**
    - In a large bowl, toss the potato wedges with olive oil until they are evenly coated.
    - Sprinkle the garlic powder, onion powder, paprika, oregano or rosemary (if using), salt, and pepper over the potatoes. Toss again to ensure all the wedges are evenly seasoned.
4. **Arrange and Bake:**
    - Spread the seasoned potato wedges in a single layer on the prepared baking sheet. Avoid overcrowding to ensure they bake evenly and become crispy.
    - Bake in the preheated oven for 25-30 minutes, flipping the wedges halfway through, until they are golden brown and crispy on the outside and tender inside.
5. **Optional Parmesan:**
    - If using Parmesan cheese, sprinkle it over the wedges during the last 5 minutes of baking for a cheesy, golden finish.
6. **Garnish and Serve:**
    - Remove the wedges from the oven and let them cool slightly. Garnish with fresh parsley or chives if desired.
    - Serve the baked potato wedges warm with your favorite dipping sauces, such as ketchup, ranch, or aioli.

Tips:

- **For Extra Crispiness:** Soak the potato wedges in cold water for 30 minutes before seasoning and baking. This helps remove excess starch and can result in a crispier texture.
- **Even Cooking:** Arrange the wedges in a single layer on the baking sheet to ensure even cooking and browning.
- **Season Variations:** Feel free to experiment with different seasonings and spices to match your taste preferences. Try adding cayenne pepper for a bit of heat or smoked paprika for a smoky flavor.

Enjoy your crispy and flavorful Baked Idaho Potato Wedges, a versatile and satisfying dish that's great for any meal!

Idaho Pork Chops

Ingredients:

- 4 bone-in or boneless pork chops (about 1-inch thick)
- 2 tablespoons olive oil
- 1 teaspoon garlic powder
- 1 teaspoon onion powder
- 1 teaspoon paprika
- 1/2 teaspoon dried thyme or rosemary
- 1/2 teaspoon ground cumin (optional, for extra depth)
- Salt and freshly ground black pepper, to taste
- 1/2 cup chicken broth
- 1 tablespoon Dijon mustard
- 1 tablespoon honey (optional, for a touch of sweetness)
- Fresh parsley, chopped, for garnish (optional)

Instructions:

1. **Prepare the Pork Chops:**
   - Pat the pork chops dry with paper towels. This helps achieve a nice sear.
   - Season both sides of the pork chops with garlic powder, onion powder, paprika, dried thyme (or rosemary), ground cumin (if using), salt, and pepper.
2. **Sear the Pork Chops:**
   - In a large skillet, heat olive oil over medium-high heat.
   - Add the pork chops and sear for 3-4 minutes per side, or until they are golden brown and have a nice crust. The internal temperature should reach 145°F (63°C). Remove the pork chops from the skillet and set aside.
3. **Make the Sauce:**
   - In the same skillet, add the chicken broth, Dijon mustard, and honey (if using). Stir to combine, scraping up any browned bits from the bottom of the pan.
   - Bring the mixture to a simmer and cook for 2-3 minutes, or until the sauce has slightly reduced and thickened.
4. **Finish Cooking:**
   - Return the pork chops to the skillet, spooning some of the sauce over them.
   - Reduce the heat to low, cover the skillet, and cook for an additional 5-7 minutes, or until the pork chops are cooked through and reach the desired internal temperature.
5. **Serve:**
   - Transfer the pork chops to serving plates and spoon the sauce over the top.
   - Garnish with chopped fresh parsley if desired.

Tips:

- **Resting the Pork Chops:** Let the pork chops rest for a few minutes after cooking before serving. This allows the juices to redistribute and helps keep the meat tender and juicy.
- **Side Dishes:** These pork chops pair well with classic sides like mashed potatoes, roasted vegetables, or a fresh salad.
- **Flavor Variations:** For different flavors, try adding a splash of white wine to the sauce or incorporating fresh herbs like rosemary or thyme.

Enjoy your Idaho Pork Chops, a savory and satisfying dish that's perfect for any dinner!

Potato and Corn Chowder

Ingredients:

- 4 large Idaho russet potatoes, peeled and diced
- 1 large onion, diced
- 2 cloves garlic, minced
- 2 cups frozen or fresh corn kernels
- 3 cups chicken or vegetable broth
- 1 cup heavy cream
- 1 cup milk
- 4 tablespoons unsalted butter
- 1/4 cup all-purpose flour
- 1 teaspoon dried thyme
- 1 teaspoon dried parsley
- Salt and freshly ground black pepper, to taste
- Optional: 1 cup cooked, crumbled bacon or diced ham
- Optional: 1 cup shredded cheddar cheese
- Optional: Fresh chives or parsley for garnish

Instructions:

1. **Prepare the Base:**
   - In a large pot, melt the butter over medium heat.
   - Add the diced onion and cook until softened and translucent, about 5 minutes.
   - Stir in the minced garlic and cook for an additional 1 minute until fragrant.
2. **Make the Roux:**
   - Sprinkle the flour over the onions and garlic. Stir well to coat and cook for about 2 minutes to remove the raw flour taste, creating a roux.
3. **Add Liquids and Potatoes:**
   - Gradually whisk in the chicken or vegetable broth, ensuring there are no lumps from the roux.
   - Add the diced potatoes and bring the mixture to a boil. Reduce the heat and let it simmer for 15-20 minutes, or until the potatoes are tender.
4. **Incorporate Corn and Cream:**
   - Stir in the corn, heavy cream, and milk. Continue to simmer for 5-10 minutes, or until the chowder is heated through and slightly thickened.
5. **Season the Chowder:**
   - Add the dried thyme, dried parsley, salt, and pepper. Adjust seasoning to taste.
6. **Add Optional Ingredients:**
   - If using, stir in the crumbled bacon or diced ham and shredded cheddar cheese until the cheese is melted and the bacon or ham is heated through.
7. **Serve:**
   - Ladle the chowder into bowls and garnish with fresh chives or parsley if desired.

- Serve hot, with crusty bread or oyster crackers on the side if desired.

Tips:

- **For Extra Creaminess:** You can use half-and-half or whole milk instead of the combination of heavy cream and milk for a richer texture.
- **Thicker Chowder:** For a thicker chowder, you can mash some of the potatoes with a fork or potato masher directly in the pot before adding the corn and cream.
- **Vegetarian Option:** Omit the bacon or ham, and use vegetable broth to keep the chowder vegetarian.

Enjoy your Potato and Corn Chowder, a warm and comforting dish that's perfect for any meal!

Idaho Potato Soup with Bacon

Ingredients:

- 4 large Idaho russet potatoes, peeled and diced
- 1 large onion, chopped
- 2 cloves garlic, minced
- 4 slices bacon, cooked and crumbled
- 3 cups chicken or vegetable broth
- 1 cup heavy cream
- 1 cup milk
- 4 tablespoons unsalted butter
- 1/4 cup all-purpose flour
- 1 teaspoon dried thyme
- 1 teaspoon dried parsley
- Salt and freshly ground black pepper, to taste
- Optional: 1 cup shredded cheddar cheese
- Optional: 1/4 cup sour cream
- Fresh chives or parsley, chopped, for garnish

Instructions:

1. **Cook the Bacon:**
    - In a large pot or Dutch oven, cook the bacon slices over medium heat until crispy. Remove the bacon from the pot and drain on paper towels. Crumble the bacon once cooled. Leave about 1-2 tablespoons of bacon fat in the pot.
2. **Sauté Onions and Garlic:**
    - Add the chopped onion to the pot with the bacon fat and cook over medium heat until softened and translucent, about 5 minutes.
    - Stir in the minced garlic and cook for an additional 1 minute until fragrant.
3. **Prepare the Roux:**
    - Melt the butter in the pot with the onions and garlic. Once melted, add the flour and stir to combine, creating a roux. Cook for about 2 minutes to remove the raw flour taste, stirring constantly.
4. **Add Liquids and Potatoes:**
    - Gradually whisk in the chicken or vegetable broth to the roux, ensuring there are no lumps.
    - Add the diced potatoes and bring the mixture to a boil. Reduce the heat and simmer for 15-20 minutes, or until the potatoes are tender.
5. **Blend the Soup (Optional):**
    - For a smoother texture, use an immersion blender to partially blend the soup directly in the pot. Alternatively, carefully transfer half of the soup to a blender, blend until smooth, and return it to the pot. If you prefer a chunkier soup, you can skip this step.

6. **Incorporate Cream and Bacon:**
    - Stir in the heavy cream and milk. Continue to simmer for 5-10 minutes until the soup is heated through and has thickened slightly.
    - Add the crumbled bacon to the soup, reserving some for garnish if desired.
7. **Season the Soup:**
    - Add the dried thyme, dried parsley, salt, and pepper. Adjust seasoning to taste.
8. **Add Optional Ingredients:**
    - If using, stir in the shredded cheddar cheese and/or sour cream until the cheese is melted and the soup is creamy.
9. **Serve:**
    - Ladle the soup into bowls and garnish with additional crumbled bacon and chopped fresh chives or parsley if desired.

Tips:

- **For Extra Creaminess:** Use all heavy cream or half-and-half instead of milk for a richer soup.
- **Thickening the Soup:** If the soup is too thin, you can mash some of the potatoes directly in the pot with a potato masher to thicken it. Alternatively, you can simmer the soup longer to reduce it to your desired thickness.
- **Toppings:** Consider adding additional toppings such as green onions, extra cheese, or croutons for added texture and flavor.

Enjoy your Idaho Potato Soup with Bacon, a rich and comforting dish that's perfect for any occasion!

Huckleberry Muffins

Ingredients:

- **For the Muffins:**
    - 1 1/2 cups all-purpose flour
    - 1/2 cup granulated sugar
    - 1/2 teaspoon salt
    - 2 teaspoons baking powder
    - 1/2 teaspoon baking soda
    - 1/2 cup unsalted butter, melted and slightly cooled
    - 1/2 cup milk (whole milk or 2% is best)
    - 2 large eggs
    - 1 teaspoon vanilla extract
    - 1 cup fresh or frozen huckleberries (if using frozen, do not thaw)
- **For the Streusel Topping (optional):**
    - 1/4 cup all-purpose flour
    - 1/4 cup granulated sugar
    - 2 tablespoons unsalted butter, cold and cut into small pieces
    - 1/2 teaspoon ground cinnamon

Instructions:

1. **Preheat Oven:**
    - Preheat your oven to 375°F (190°C). Line a 12-cup muffin tin with paper liners or lightly grease it.
2. **Prepare the Streusel Topping (optional):**
    - In a small bowl, mix together the flour, sugar, and cinnamon. Cut in the cold butter with a pastry cutter or your fingers until the mixture resembles coarse crumbs. Set aside.
3. **Mix Dry Ingredients:**
    - In a large bowl, whisk together the flour, sugar, salt, baking powder, and baking soda.
4. **Combine Wet Ingredients:**
    - In another bowl, whisk together the melted butter, milk, eggs, and vanilla extract.
5. **Combine Wet and Dry Ingredients:**
    - Pour the wet ingredients into the dry ingredients and stir until just combined. Do not overmix; the batter should be lumpy.
6. **Fold in Huckleberries:**
    - Gently fold the huckleberries into the batter. If using frozen huckleberries, fold them in gently to avoid coloring the batter too much.
7. **Fill Muffin Tin:**
    - Divide the batter evenly among the muffin cups, filling each about 2/3 full. If using the streusel topping, sprinkle a generous amount on top of each muffin.

8. **Bake:**
   - Bake in the preheated oven for 18-22 minutes, or until a toothpick inserted into the center of a muffin comes out clean.
9. **Cool and Serve:**
   - Allow the muffins to cool in the tin for 5 minutes, then transfer them to a wire rack to cool completely.

Tips:

- **Avoid Overmixing:** Mix the batter just until the ingredients are combined to ensure tender muffins.
- **Frozen Huckleberries:** If using frozen huckleberries, fold them in gently to minimize bleeding. You can also toss them in a bit of flour before adding them to the batter to help prevent them from sinking.
- **Storage:** Store muffins in an airtight container at room temperature for up to 3 days, or freeze for longer storage. Reheat frozen muffins in the microwave or oven before serving.

Enjoy your Huckleberry Muffins, a delicious and fruity treat that's sure to brighten your day!

Herbed Potato Gratin

Ingredients:

- **For the Gratin:**
    - 2 pounds Idaho russet potatoes (about 4-5 medium-sized)
    - 1 cup grated Gruyère cheese (or a mix of Gruyère and Parmesan)
    - 1 cup grated Parmesan cheese
    - 2 cups heavy cream
    - 1 cup whole milk
    - 3 cloves garlic, minced
    - 2 tablespoons unsalted butter
    - 1 tablespoon all-purpose flour
    - 1 teaspoon dried thyme (or 1 tablespoon fresh thyme, chopped)
    - 1 teaspoon dried rosemary (or 1 tablespoon fresh rosemary, chopped)
    - Salt and freshly ground black pepper, to taste
    - Optional: 1/2 cup chopped fresh parsley for garnish

Instructions:

1. **Preheat Oven:**
    - Preheat your oven to 375°F (190°C). Grease a 9x13-inch baking dish or a similar-sized casserole dish with butter or non-stick spray.
2. **Prepare the Potatoes:**
    - Peel the potatoes and slice them thinly (about 1/8-inch thick) using a mandoline or a sharp knife. Place the sliced potatoes in a bowl of cold water to prevent browning.
3. **Make the Sauce:**
    - In a medium saucepan, melt the butter over medium heat. Add the minced garlic and cook for 1 minute until fragrant.
    - Stir in the flour and cook for another 1-2 minutes, whisking constantly to form a roux.
    - Gradually whisk in the heavy cream and milk, ensuring the mixture is smooth and free of lumps.
    - Add the dried thyme, dried rosemary, salt, and pepper. Cook, stirring frequently, until the sauce thickens slightly, about 5-7 minutes. Remove from heat.
4. **Assemble the Gratin:**
    - Drain the potato slices and pat them dry with paper towels.
    - Layer half of the potato slices in the bottom of the prepared baking dish, overlapping them slightly.
    - Pour half of the sauce over the first layer of potatoes and sprinkle with half of the Gruyère and Parmesan cheeses.
    - Add the remaining potato slices in another layer, pour the remaining sauce over the top, and sprinkle with the remaining cheeses.

5. **Bake the Gratin:**
    - Cover the baking dish with aluminum foil and bake in the preheated oven for 45 minutes.
    - Remove the foil and bake for an additional 20-25 minutes, or until the top is golden brown and the potatoes are tender when pierced with a fork.
6. **Garnish and Serve:**
    - Let the gratin cool for 10-15 minutes before serving. Garnish with chopped fresh parsley if desired.

Tips:

- **Even Slicing:** Slice the potatoes as evenly as possible to ensure they cook uniformly.
- **Make Ahead:** You can assemble the gratin a day in advance. Cover it with foil and refrigerate until ready to bake. Increase the baking time by 10-15 minutes if baking from cold.
- **Texture:** For a crispier top, you can broil the gratin for a few minutes after baking.

Enjoy your Herbed Potato Gratin, a creamy and cheesy side dish that's perfect for any occasion!

Idaho Style Potato Hash

Ingredients:

- 4 large Idaho russet potatoes
- 1 large onion, diced
- 1 bell pepper (any color), diced
- 2 cloves garlic, minced
- 1/2 cup diced cooked ham or bacon (optional, for added flavor)
- 2 tablespoons olive oil or vegetable oil
- 1 teaspoon paprika
- 1/2 teaspoon ground cumin
- 1/2 teaspoon dried thyme or rosemary
- Salt and freshly ground black pepper, to taste
- 2 tablespoons fresh parsley or chives, chopped (for garnish)
- Optional: 2-3 large eggs (for serving)

Instructions:

1. **Prepare the Potatoes:**
   - Peel the potatoes (if desired) and cut them into small, evenly-sized cubes (about 1/2-inch).
2. **Cook the Potatoes:**
   - Place the cubed potatoes in a large pot and cover with water. Add a pinch of salt.
   - Bring to a boil, then reduce the heat and simmer for 5-7 minutes, or until the potatoes are just tender but still firm (not mushy). Drain and set aside.
3. **Sauté Vegetables and Meat:**
   - In a large skillet, heat the olive oil over medium heat.
   - Add the diced onion and bell pepper. Cook, stirring occasionally, until the vegetables are softened and slightly caramelized, about 5-7 minutes.
   - Stir in the minced garlic and cook for an additional 1 minute.
4. **Add the Potatoes and Seasonings:**
   - Add the cooked potato cubes to the skillet, along with the paprika, ground cumin, and dried thyme or rosemary.
   - Cook, stirring occasionally, until the potatoes are golden brown and crispy on the edges, about 10-15 minutes. If using ham or bacon, stir it in during the last few minutes of cooking to heat through and add extra flavor.
5. **Season and Garnish:**
   - Season the hash with salt and freshly ground black pepper to taste.
   - Garnish with chopped fresh parsley or chives.
6. **Optional: Serve with Eggs:**
   - If desired, you can serve the hash with eggs cooked to your liking (fried, poached, or scrambled). To do this, cook the eggs in a separate skillet while the hash is finishing up, then serve on top or alongside the potato hash.

Tips:

- **Crispy Texture:** For extra crispy potatoes, make sure the potatoes are well-drained and patted dry before adding them to the skillet.
- **Flavor Variations:** Feel free to add other vegetables like mushrooms, zucchini, or spinach, or swap the ham or bacon for sausage or chorizo.
- **Make Ahead:** You can prepare the potatoes and vegetables in advance and store them in the refrigerator. Reheat them in the skillet before serving for a quick meal.

Enjoy your Idaho Style Potato Hash, a versatile and satisfying dish that's perfect for any meal of the day!

Classic Potato and Chive Soup

Ingredients:

- 4 large Idaho russet potatoes, peeled and diced
- 1 large onion, chopped
- 2 cloves garlic, minced
- 4 cups chicken or vegetable broth
- 1 cup heavy cream (or half-and-half for a lighter version)
- 2 tablespoons unsalted butter
- 1/4 cup all-purpose flour
- 1 teaspoon dried thyme or 1 tablespoon fresh thyme, chopped
- Salt and freshly ground black pepper, to taste
- 1/2 cup fresh chives, chopped (plus extra for garnish)
- Optional: 1/2 cup grated cheddar cheese (for added richness)
- Optional: 4 slices bacon, cooked and crumbled (for topping)

Instructions:

1. **Prepare the Potatoes:**
   - Peel and dice the potatoes into small, even pieces.
2. **Cook the Vegetables:**
   - In a large pot or Dutch oven, melt the butter over medium heat.
   - Add the chopped onion and cook until softened and translucent, about 5 minutes.
   - Stir in the minced garlic and cook for an additional 1 minute.
3. **Make the Roux:**
   - Sprinkle the flour over the onions and garlic. Stir well to combine and cook for about 2 minutes, creating a roux. This will help thicken the soup.
4. **Add Liquids and Potatoes:**
   - Gradually whisk in the chicken or vegetable broth, ensuring there are no lumps.
   - Add the diced potatoes and bring the mixture to a boil. Reduce the heat and simmer for 15-20 minutes, or until the potatoes are tender.
5. **Blend the Soup (Optional):**
   - For a smoother texture, use an immersion blender to partially or fully blend the soup directly in the pot. Alternatively, transfer half of the soup to a blender, blend until smooth, and return it to the pot.
6. **Incorporate Cream and Chives:**
   - Stir in the heavy cream (or half-and-half) and continue to heat the soup until warmed through.
   - Add the chopped fresh chives, and season with dried thyme, salt, and pepper to taste.
   - If using, stir in the grated cheddar cheese until melted and incorporated.
7. **Serve:**
   - Ladle the soup into bowls and garnish with additional fresh chives and crumbled bacon if desired.

Tips:

- **Texture:** Adjust the texture of the soup by blending more or less, depending on your preference for a chunky or smooth soup.
- **Flavor Enhancements:** For extra flavor, consider adding a splash of white wine or a squeeze of lemon juice to the soup.
- **Toppings:** Top with extra cheese, croutons, or a drizzle of cream for added richness.

Enjoy your Classic Potato and Chive Soup, a delicious and warming dish perfect for any time of the year!

Huckleberry Smoothie

Ingredients:

- 1 cup fresh or frozen huckleberries (if using frozen, do not thaw)
- 1 banana, peeled and sliced
- 1 cup Greek yogurt (plain or vanilla)
- 1/2 cup milk (or any non-dairy milk like almond, soy, or oat milk)
- 1 tablespoon honey or maple syrup (adjust to taste)
- 1/2 teaspoon vanilla extract
- Optional: 1 tablespoon chia seeds or flaxseeds (for added fiber and nutrients)
- Optional: 1/2 cup spinach or kale (for an extra boost of greens)
- Optional: Ice cubes (if using fresh huckleberries and you prefer a colder, thicker smoothie)

Instructions:

1. **Prepare Ingredients:**
   - If using fresh huckleberries, rinse them thoroughly under cold water. If using frozen huckleberries, you can add them directly to the blender.
2. **Blend Smoothie:**
   - In a blender, combine the huckleberries, banana, Greek yogurt, milk, honey or maple syrup, and vanilla extract.
   - Blend until smooth and creamy. If the smoothie is too thick, you can add more milk to reach your desired consistency.
3. **Add Optional Ingredients:**
   - If using, add chia seeds or flaxseeds and blend for a few more seconds to incorporate.
   - For a green boost, add spinach or kale and blend until fully combined.
   - If you prefer a colder smoothie, add ice cubes and blend until the ice is crushed and the smoothie is frothy.
4. **Serve:**
   - Pour the smoothie into glasses and serve immediately. Garnish with a few whole huckleberries or a sprig of mint if desired.

Tips:

- **Sweetness:** Adjust the sweetness to your taste by adding more honey or maple syrup if needed.
- **Texture:** For a thicker smoothie, use frozen huckleberries or add more Greek yogurt. For a thinner smoothie, increase the amount of milk.
- **Variations:** Experiment with different fruits like blueberries or raspberries for a different flavor profile.

Enjoy your Huckleberry Smoothie, a delicious and nutritious drink that's packed with flavor and goodness!

Bacon and Cheddar Potato Skins

Ingredients:

- 4 large Idaho russet potatoes
- 4 slices bacon
- 1 cup shredded cheddar cheese
- 1/2 cup sour cream
- 1/4 cup chopped fresh chives or green onions
- 1 tablespoon olive oil
- Salt and freshly ground black pepper, to taste
- Optional: 1/4 teaspoon garlic powder
- Optional: 1/4 teaspoon smoked paprika

Instructions:

1. **Preheat Oven:**
   - Preheat your oven to 400°F (200°C).
2. **Bake the Potatoes:**
   - Scrub the potatoes clean and pat them dry. Pierce each potato a few times with a fork.
   - Place the potatoes directly on the oven rack and bake for 45-60 minutes, or until tender when pierced with a fork. Let them cool slightly.
3. **Prepare the Bacon:**
   - While the potatoes are baking, cook the bacon in a skillet over medium heat until crispy. Remove the bacon from the skillet and drain on paper towels. Once cooled, crumble the bacon into small pieces.
4. **Prepare the Potato Skins:**
   - Once the potatoes are cool enough to handle, cut them in half lengthwise.
   - Using a spoon, carefully scoop out most of the flesh, leaving about 1/4 inch of potato inside the skin. You can save the potato flesh for another use, like mashed potatoes.
   - Brush the inside and outside of the potato skins with olive oil and season with salt, pepper, and optional garlic powder and smoked paprika.
5. **Crisp the Potato Skins:**
   - Place the potato skins on a baking sheet, cut side up.
   - Bake in the preheated oven for about 10 minutes. Flip the skins over and bake for an additional 10 minutes, or until the edges are crispy.
6. **Add Toppings:**
   - Remove the potato skins from the oven and sprinkle each skin with shredded cheddar cheese and crumbled bacon.
   - Return to the oven and bake for another 5-7 minutes, or until the cheese is melted and bubbly.
7. **Garnish and Serve:**
   - Remove the potato skins from the oven and let them cool slightly.

- Top each potato skin with a dollop of sour cream and a sprinkle of chopped chives or green onions.

Tips:

- **Crispier Skins:** For extra crispy skins, you can broil them for 1-2 minutes after baking. Watch closely to avoid burning.
- **Cheese Variations:** Try using different types of cheese like Monterey Jack, pepper jack, or a cheese blend for varied flavors.
- **Toppings:** Customize your potato skins with additional toppings such as jalapeños, olives, or diced tomatoes if desired.

Enjoy your Bacon and Cheddar Potato Skins, a deliciously crispy and cheesy treat that's sure to be a hit with everyone!

Idaho Trout with Lemon Butter

Ingredients:

- 4 Idaho trout fillets (about 6 ounces each)
- Salt and freshly ground black pepper, to taste
- 2 tablespoons all-purpose flour (for dredging)
- 3 tablespoons unsalted butter
- 2 tablespoons olive oil
- 2 cloves garlic, minced
- 1/4 cup white wine (or chicken broth)
- Juice of 1 lemon (about 2 tablespoons)
- 1 tablespoon lemon zest
- 2 tablespoons capers (optional)
- 2 tablespoons fresh parsley, chopped (for garnish)
- Lemon wedges (for serving)

Instructions:

1. **Prepare the Trout:**
    - Pat the trout fillets dry with paper towels. Season both sides with salt and black pepper.
    - Dredge each fillet lightly in flour, shaking off any excess.
2. **Cook the Trout:**
    - In a large skillet, heat the olive oil over medium-high heat.
    - Add the trout fillets, skin side down if they have skin, and cook for 3-4 minutes per side, or until the fish is golden brown and cooked through. The fish should flake easily with a fork. Transfer the cooked fillets to a plate and keep warm.
3. **Make the Lemon Butter Sauce:**
    - In the same skillet, reduce the heat to medium. Add the butter and let it melt.
    - Add the minced garlic and cook for about 1 minute, until fragrant but not browned.
    - Pour in the white wine (or chicken broth) and lemon juice, scraping up any browned bits from the bottom of the skillet.
    - Stir in the lemon zest and capers (if using). Cook for 2-3 minutes, or until the sauce has reduced slightly and thickened.
4. **Finish the Dish:**
    - Return the trout fillets to the skillet, spooning some of the sauce over the top. Heat for another 1-2 minutes, or until the trout is warmed through.
5. **Serve:**
    - Transfer the trout fillets to serving plates. Spoon the lemon butter sauce over the top.
    - Garnish with chopped fresh parsley and serve with lemon wedges on the side.

Tips:

- **Skin-on Trout:** If using skin-on trout, cook the skin side down first to get it crispy before flipping.
- **Wine Substitute:** If you prefer not to use wine, you can substitute with additional chicken broth or a splash of water.
- **Vegetable Side:** Serve with a side of steamed vegetables or a light salad for a complete meal.

Enjoy your Idaho Trout with Lemon Butter, a simple yet elegant dish that brings out the best in fresh trout with a delightful lemony twist!

Potato and Green Bean Salad

Ingredients:

- **For the Salad:**
    - 1 1/2 pounds small potatoes (such as Yukon Gold or baby red potatoes)
    - 8 ounces green beans, trimmed and cut into bite-sized pieces
    - 1/4 cup red onion, finely diced
    - 1/4 cup chopped fresh parsley (or dill, if preferred)
    - Optional: 1/4 cup crumbled feta cheese or sliced black olives for added flavor
- **For the Dressing:**
    - 1/4 cup extra-virgin olive oil
    - 2 tablespoons red wine vinegar (or white wine vinegar)
    - 1 tablespoon Dijon mustard
    - 1 teaspoon honey or maple syrup
    - 1 clove garlic, minced
    - Salt and freshly ground black pepper, to taste

Instructions:

1. **Cook the Potatoes:**
    - Wash and scrub the potatoes. Cut them into bite-sized chunks if they are large.
    - Place the potatoes in a large pot and cover with cold water. Add a pinch of salt.
    - Bring to a boil over high heat, then reduce to a simmer. Cook until the potatoes are tender when pierced with a fork, about 10-12 minutes.
    - Drain and let the potatoes cool slightly.
2. **Cook the Green Beans:**
    - While the potatoes are cooking, bring a small pot of water to a boil.
    - Add the green beans and cook for 3-4 minutes, or until bright green and tender-crisp.
    - Drain the green beans and immediately transfer them to a bowl of ice water to stop the cooking process. Once cooled, drain again.
3. **Prepare the Dressing:**
    - In a small bowl, whisk together the olive oil, red wine vinegar, Dijon mustard, honey or maple syrup, minced garlic, salt, and pepper until well combined.
4. **Assemble the Salad:**
    - In a large mixing bowl, combine the cooked potatoes, green beans, diced red onion, and chopped parsley.
    - Pour the dressing over the salad and toss gently to coat all the ingredients evenly.
    - If using, gently fold in the crumbled feta cheese or sliced black olives.
5. **Chill and Serve:**
    - Cover the salad and refrigerate for at least 30 minutes to allow the flavors to meld. This salad can be made a day in advance.

- Before serving, give the salad a gentle toss and adjust the seasoning with additional salt and pepper if needed.

Tips:

- **Potato Type:** Small waxy potatoes hold their shape well in salads, but you can use other varieties if preferred.
- **Make Ahead:** This salad keeps well in the refrigerator for up to 3 days, making it a great option for meal prep or make-ahead gatherings.
- **Additions:** Feel free to customize with other ingredients like cherry tomatoes, sliced radishes, or bacon bits for added flavor.

Enjoy your Potato and Green Bean Salad, a versatile and tasty dish that's perfect for any occasion!

Huckleberry Barbecue Sauce

Ingredients:

- 1 cup fresh or frozen huckleberries (thawed if frozen)
- 1 cup ketchup
- 1/2 cup apple cider vinegar
- 1/4 cup honey or maple syrup
- 1/4 cup brown sugar
- 2 tablespoons Worcestershire sauce
- 2 tablespoons soy sauce
- 1 tablespoon Dijon mustard
- 1 teaspoon smoked paprika
- 1/2 teaspoon ground black pepper
- 1/2 teaspoon garlic powder
- 1/2 teaspoon onion powder
- Optional: 1/4 teaspoon cayenne pepper (for a spicy kick)

Instructions:

1. **Prepare the Huckleberries:**
   - If using fresh huckleberries, rinse them under cold water. If using frozen huckleberries, thaw them first and drain any excess liquid.
2. **Cook the Sauce:**
   - In a medium saucepan, combine the huckleberries, ketchup, apple cider vinegar, honey or maple syrup, brown sugar, Worcestershire sauce, soy sauce, and Dijon mustard.
   - Stir well to combine and bring the mixture to a simmer over medium heat.
3. **Season the Sauce:**
   - Add the smoked paprika, ground black pepper, garlic powder, onion powder, and optional cayenne pepper.
   - Stir well and let the sauce simmer for 15-20 minutes, stirring occasionally, until it has thickened slightly and the flavors have melded together.
4. **Blend the Sauce:**
   - For a smoother texture, use an immersion blender to blend the sauce directly in the pot. Alternatively, let the sauce cool slightly and blend it in a regular blender or food processor. Be careful with hot liquids when blending.
5. **Adjust and Cool:**
   - Taste the sauce and adjust the seasoning if needed, adding more honey or vinegar to balance the sweetness and tanginess to your liking.
   - Let the sauce cool to room temperature. It will continue to thicken as it cools.
6. **Store and Serve:**
   - Transfer the cooled barbecue sauce to a clean jar or airtight container.
   - Refrigerate for up to 2 weeks. The sauce can also be frozen for up to 3 months.

Tips:

- **Huckleberry Substitution:** If huckleberries are not available, you can substitute with blueberries for a similar but slightly different flavor profile.
- **Sweetness and Spice:** Adjust the sweetness and spiciness of the sauce by varying the amount of honey or cayenne pepper to suit your taste.
- **Uses:** This barbecue sauce is great for grilling chicken, pork, or ribs, or as a flavorful dipping sauce for vegetables and appetizers.

Enjoy your Huckleberry Barbecue Sauce, a delicious and distinctive addition to your culinary repertoire!

Idaho Beef and Potato Casserole

Ingredients:

- **For the Casserole:**
    - 1 pound ground beef
    - 4 large Idaho russet potatoes, peeled and thinly sliced
    - 1 large onion, chopped
    - 2 cloves garlic, minced
    - 1 cup frozen peas (or any vegetable of your choice)
    - 1 cup shredded cheddar cheese (or your preferred cheese)
    - 2 tablespoons olive oil
    - 1 teaspoon dried thyme
    - 1 teaspoon dried rosemary
    - Salt and freshly ground black pepper, to taste
- **For the Sauce:**
    - 2 tablespoons unsalted butter
    - 2 tablespoons all-purpose flour
    - 1 1/2 cups beef broth
    - 1/2 cup milk or heavy cream
    - 1 tablespoon Worcestershire sauce
    - 1/2 teaspoon garlic powder
    - 1/4 teaspoon onion powder
    - 1/4 teaspoon paprika

Instructions:

1. **Prepare the Potatoes:**
    - Preheat your oven to 375°F (190°C).
    - Peel and thinly slice the potatoes (about 1/8-inch thick). Place the slices in a bowl of cold water to prevent browning.
2. **Cook the Beef:**
    - In a large skillet, heat olive oil over medium-high heat.
    - Add the chopped onion and cook until softened, about 5 minutes.
    - Add the minced garlic and cook for 1 minute more.
    - Add the ground beef, breaking it up with a spoon. Cook until browned and cooked through, about 7-10 minutes. Drain any excess fat.
    - Stir in the frozen peas, dried thyme, dried rosemary, salt, and pepper. Cook for an additional 2 minutes. Remove from heat and set aside.
3. **Prepare the Sauce:**
    - In a medium saucepan, melt the butter over medium heat.
    - Stir in the flour and cook for about 1 minute, creating a roux.
    - Gradually whisk in the beef broth and milk, ensuring there are no lumps.

- Add the Worcestershire sauce, garlic powder, onion powder, and paprika. Continue to cook, whisking frequently, until the sauce has thickened, about 5 minutes.

4. **Assemble the Casserole:**
   - Grease a 9x13-inch baking dish or similar sized casserole dish.
   - Spread a layer of sliced potatoes on the bottom of the dish. Season with salt and pepper.
   - Spread the cooked beef mixture evenly over the potatoes.
   - Pour the prepared sauce over the beef mixture, spreading it out evenly.
   - Top with a final layer of sliced potatoes. Season the top layer with salt and pepper.
   - Sprinkle shredded cheddar cheese evenly over the top.

5. **Bake the Casserole:**
   - Cover the dish with aluminum foil and bake in the preheated oven for 45 minutes.
   - Remove the foil and bake for an additional 15-20 minutes, or until the potatoes are tender and the cheese is bubbly and golden brown.

6. **Cool and Serve:**
   - Let the casserole cool for a few minutes before serving to allow it to set.

Tips:

- **Potato Slicing:** Thinly slicing the potatoes ensures they cook evenly and become tender.
- **Vegetable Variations:** Feel free to use other vegetables like carrots, corn, or green beans in place of peas.
- **Make Ahead:** This casserole can be assembled ahead of time and stored in the refrigerator for up to 24 hours before baking.

Enjoy your Idaho Beef and Potato Casserole, a comforting and delicious dish that's perfect for a satisfying meal!

Garlic Mashed Potatoes

Ingredients:

- 2 pounds Idaho russet potatoes, peeled and cut into chunks
- 1 head garlic
- 1/4 cup unsalted butter, plus extra for roasting garlic
- 1/2 cup milk (or heavy cream for extra richness)
- Salt and freshly ground black pepper, to taste
- Optional: 2 tablespoons chopped fresh chives or parsley (for garnish)

Instructions:

1. **Prepare the Garlic:**
    - Preheat your oven to 400°F (200°C).
    - Slice the top off the head of garlic to expose the individual cloves.
    - Drizzle with a small amount of olive oil and wrap the garlic head in aluminum foil.
    - Roast in the preheated oven for 35-40 minutes, or until the cloves are soft and caramelized. Let cool slightly, then squeeze the cloves out of their skins and set aside.
2. **Cook the Potatoes:**
    - Place the peeled and cut potatoes in a large pot and cover with cold water. Add a pinch of salt.
    - Bring to a boil over high heat, then reduce to a simmer and cook until the potatoes are tender and easily pierced with a fork, about 15-20 minutes.
    - Drain the potatoes and return them to the pot or a large mixing bowl.
3. **Mash the Potatoes:**
    - Add the butter to the hot potatoes and mash until smooth.
    - Stir in the roasted garlic, either by mashing it with the potatoes or by mixing it in thoroughly.
4. **Add Milk and Season:**
    - Gradually stir in the milk (or heavy cream) until the potatoes reach your desired consistency.
    - Season with salt and pepper to taste. Mix well.
5. **Garnish and Serve:**
    - Transfer the mashed potatoes to a serving dish.
    - Optionally, garnish with chopped fresh chives or parsley for a touch of color and added flavor.

Tips:

- **Creaminess:** For extra creamy mashed potatoes, you can use heavy cream or half-and-half instead of milk.
- **Butter:** Using room temperature butter helps it blend in more smoothly with the potatoes.

- **Garlic:** Adjust the amount of roasted garlic to your taste. For a milder garlic flavor, use fewer cloves.

Enjoy your Garlic Mashed Potatoes, a comforting and flavorful side that's sure to be a hit at your table!

Huckleberry Cobbler

Ingredients:

- **For the Filling:**
    - 4 cups fresh or frozen huckleberries (thawed and drained if frozen)
    - 1 cup granulated sugar
    - 1/4 cup cornstarch
    - 1 tablespoon lemon juice
    - 1 teaspoon vanilla extract
    - 1/2 teaspoon ground cinnamon (optional)
    - 1/4 teaspoon salt
- **For the Topping:**
    - 1 1/2 cups all-purpose flour
    - 1/4 cup granulated sugar
    - 1/4 cup packed brown sugar
    - 1/2 teaspoon baking powder
    - 1/4 teaspoon baking soda
    - 1/4 teaspoon salt
    - 1/2 cup cold unsalted butter, cut into small cubes
    - 1/2 cup buttermilk (or regular milk with 1 tablespoon lemon juice or vinegar added)
    - 1 teaspoon vanilla extract
    - Optional: 1 tablespoon coarse sugar for sprinkling on top

Instructions:

1. **Preheat Oven:**
    - Preheat your oven to 375°F (190°C).
2. **Prepare the Filling:**
    - In a large bowl, combine the huckleberries, granulated sugar, cornstarch, lemon juice, vanilla extract, ground cinnamon (if using), and salt. Stir well to combine.
    - Transfer the huckleberry mixture to a 9x13-inch baking dish or a similar-sized ovenproof dish.
3. **Prepare the Topping:**
    - In a medium bowl, whisk together the flour, granulated sugar, brown sugar, baking powder, baking soda, and salt.
    - Cut in the cold butter using a pastry cutter or your fingers until the mixture resembles coarse crumbs.
    - Stir in the buttermilk and vanilla extract until just combined. Be careful not to overmix; the dough should be somewhat lumpy.
4. **Assemble the Cobbler:**
    - Drop spoonfuls of the biscuit topping over the huckleberry filling, covering most of the surface. It's okay if some of the filling shows through.
5. **Bake the Cobbler:**

- - Sprinkle the top with coarse sugar if desired.
  - Bake in the preheated oven for 35-45 minutes, or until the topping is golden brown and the filling is bubbling.
6. **Cool and Serve:**
    - Allow the cobbler to cool slightly before serving. It can be served warm or at room temperature.
    - Serve with a scoop of vanilla ice cream or a dollop of whipped cream if desired.

Tips:

- **Huckleberries:** If huckleberries are not available, you can substitute with blueberries, blackberries, or a mix of berries.
- **Buttermilk Substitute:** If you don't have buttermilk, you can use regular milk with a tablespoon of lemon juice or vinegar mixed in.
- **Topping Texture:** For a more even topping, spread the biscuit dough out with a spatula or the back of a spoon.

Enjoy your Huckleberry Cobbler, a delightful and comforting dessert that brings out the best in fresh huckleberries!

Idaho Chicken and Potato Bake

Ingredients:

- **For the Bake:**
    - 4 boneless, skinless chicken thighs or breasts
    - 1 1/2 pounds Idaho potatoes, peeled and cut into 1-inch cubes
    - 1 large onion, chopped
    - 3 cloves garlic, minced
    - 1 cup baby carrots (optional)
    - 1 cup shredded cheddar cheese (optional)
    - 2 tablespoons olive oil
    - 1 teaspoon dried thyme
    - 1 teaspoon dried rosemary
    - Salt and freshly ground black pepper, to taste
- **For the Sauce:**
    - 1/2 cup chicken broth
    - 1/2 cup heavy cream or milk
    - 2 tablespoons Dijon mustard
    - 1 tablespoon Worcestershire sauce
    - 1 tablespoon all-purpose flour (optional, for thickening)

Instructions:

1. **Preheat Oven:**
    - Preheat your oven to 400°F (200°C).
2. **Prepare the Vegetables:**
    - In a large bowl, toss the cubed potatoes, chopped onion, and baby carrots (if using) with 1 tablespoon of olive oil, dried thyme, dried rosemary, salt, and pepper until evenly coated.
3. **Prepare the Chicken:**
    - Rub the chicken pieces with the remaining 1 tablespoon of olive oil and season with salt and pepper.
4. **Assemble the Bake:**
    - Spread the seasoned potatoes and vegetables evenly in a large baking dish.
    - Place the chicken pieces on top of the vegetables.
5. **Prepare the Sauce:**
    - In a small bowl, whisk together the chicken broth, heavy cream (or milk), Dijon mustard, and Worcestershire sauce. If you prefer a thicker sauce, whisk in 1 tablespoon of flour to the mixture.
    - Pour the sauce evenly over the chicken and vegetables in the baking dish.
6. **Bake:**
    - Cover the baking dish with aluminum foil and bake in the preheated oven for 35-40 minutes.

- Remove the foil and bake for an additional 15-20 minutes, or until the chicken is cooked through (internal temperature should reach 165°F or 74°C) and the potatoes are tender.
7. **Add Cheese (Optional):**
    - If using cheese, sprinkle shredded cheddar cheese over the top of the casserole during the last 10 minutes of baking, and return to the oven until the cheese is melted and bubbly.
8. **Serve:**
    - Let the casserole rest for a few minutes before serving. Garnish with fresh herbs if desired.

Tips:

- **Chicken:** If you prefer, you can use bone-in, skin-on chicken pieces for extra flavor. Just adjust the cooking time as needed.
- **Vegetables:** Feel free to add other vegetables like bell peppers or green beans to customize the dish.
- **Sauce Thickness:** Adjust the thickness of the sauce by adding or reducing the amount of flour.

Enjoy your Idaho Chicken and Potato Bake, a satisfying and easy-to-make meal that's perfect for any night of the week!

Potato and Spinach Frittata

Ingredients:

- **For the Frittata:**
    - 1 tablespoon olive oil
    - 1 medium potato, peeled and thinly sliced (about 1/8-inch thick)
    - 1 small onion, diced
    - 2 cloves garlic, minced
    - 2 cups fresh spinach leaves, chopped
    - 6 large eggs
    - 1/2 cup milk (or heavy cream for a richer taste)
    - 1/2 cup shredded cheese (cheddar, feta, or your choice)
    - Salt and freshly ground black pepper, to taste
    - Optional: 1/4 teaspoon crushed red pepper flakes (for a bit of heat)
    - Optional: Fresh herbs (such as chives or parsley) for garnish

Instructions:

1. **Prepare the Potatoes:**
    - Heat the olive oil in a 10-inch oven-safe skillet (cast iron works great) over medium heat.
    - Add the sliced potatoes and cook, stirring occasionally, until tender and golden brown, about 10-12 minutes. Remove the potatoes from the skillet and set aside.
2. **Cook the Vegetables:**
    - In the same skillet, add the diced onion and cook until softened, about 5 minutes.
    - Add the minced garlic and cook for an additional minute, until fragrant.
    - Add the chopped spinach and cook until wilted, about 2 minutes. Return the cooked potatoes to the skillet and mix well.
3. **Prepare the Egg Mixture:**
    - In a large bowl, whisk together the eggs, milk, salt, pepper, and crushed red pepper flakes (if using).
    - Stir in the shredded cheese.
4. **Combine and Cook:**
    - Pour the egg mixture over the cooked vegetables and potatoes in the skillet. Stir gently to combine.
    - Cook over medium heat until the edges start to set, about 5 minutes.
5. **Bake the Frittata:**
    - Transfer the skillet to the preheated oven and bake for 15-20 minutes, or until the frittata is fully set and the top is golden brown. You can test for doneness by inserting a knife in the center; it should come out clean.
6. **Cool and Serve:**
    - Let the frittata cool for a few minutes before slicing.
    - Garnish with fresh herbs if desired and serve warm or at room temperature.

Tips:

- **Vegetable Variations:** Feel free to add other vegetables like bell peppers, mushrooms, or tomatoes based on your preference.
- **Cheese Choices:** Experiment with different cheeses such as goat cheese, mozzarella, or Parmesan for different flavor profiles.
- **Cooking Ahead:** Frittatas are great for make-ahead meals and can be stored in the refrigerator for up to 3 days. Reheat gently in the oven or microwave.

Enjoy your Potato and Spinach Frittata, a versatile and satisfying dish that's perfect for any time of day!

Huckleberry Ice Cream

Ingredients:

- 2 cups fresh or frozen huckleberries (thawed and drained if frozen)
- 1 cup granulated sugar
- 1 cup whole milk
- 1 cup heavy cream
- 1 teaspoon vanilla extract
- 1 tablespoon lemon juice
- 1/4 teaspoon salt

Instructions:

1. **Prepare the Huckleberries:**
    - If using fresh huckleberries, rinse them under cold water. If using frozen huckleberries, thaw them first and drain any excess liquid.
    - In a medium bowl, combine the huckleberries with 1/4 cup of the granulated sugar. Mash the berries slightly with a fork or potato masher, leaving some chunks for texture. Set aside.
2. **Make the Ice Cream Base:**
    - In a separate large bowl, whisk together the remaining 3/4 cup of granulated sugar and the salt with the milk until the sugar is dissolved.
    - Stir in the heavy cream, vanilla extract, and lemon juice. Mix well.
3. **Combine and Chill:**
    - Gently fold the huckleberry mixture into the ice cream base, making sure it's evenly distributed.
    - Cover the mixture and refrigerate for at least 2 hours, or until thoroughly chilled. This step helps improve the texture and flavor.
4. **Churn the Ice Cream:**
    - Pour the chilled mixture into an ice cream maker and churn according to the manufacturer's instructions, typically for 20-30 minutes, or until it reaches a soft-serve consistency.
5. **Freeze:**
    - Transfer the churned ice cream to an airtight container and freeze for at least 2 hours, or until firm.
6. **Serve:**
    - Scoop and serve the huckleberry ice cream as a refreshing dessert.

Tips:

- **Ice Cream Maker:** If you don't have an ice cream maker, you can use a no-churn method by placing the mixture in a freezer-safe container and stirring every 30 minutes for the first 2-3 hours to break up ice crystals.

- **Texture:** For a smoother texture, strain the huckleberry mixture through a fine-mesh sieve before adding it to the ice cream base.
- **Mix-ins:** Consider adding small chunks of huckleberries or a swirl of huckleberry sauce for extra texture and flavor.

Enjoy your Huckleberry Ice Cream, a delightful and unique treat that showcases the special flavor of huckleberries!

Potato and Sausage Stew

Ingredients:

- **For the Stew:**
    - 1 pound (450g) sausage (such as Italian, kielbasa, or chorizo), sliced into rounds
    - 1 tablespoon olive oil
    - 1 large onion, chopped
    - 3 cloves garlic, minced
    - 3 large potatoes, peeled and diced (about 1-inch cubes)
    - 3 carrots, peeled and sliced
    - 2 celery stalks, sliced
    - 1 bell pepper, chopped (optional)
    - 1 cup green beans, cut into 1-inch pieces (optional)
    - 4 cups chicken or vegetable broth
    - 1 cup diced tomatoes (canned or fresh)
    - 1 teaspoon dried thyme
    - 1 teaspoon dried oregano
    - 1 bay leaf
    - Salt and freshly ground black pepper, to taste
    - 2 tablespoons chopped fresh parsley (for garnish)

Instructions:

1. **Cook the Sausage:**
    - In a large pot or Dutch oven, heat the olive oil over medium heat.
    - Add the sliced sausage and cook until browned and slightly crispy, about 5-7 minutes. Remove the sausage from the pot and set aside.
2. **Sauté the Vegetables:**
    - In the same pot, add the chopped onion and cook until softened, about 5 minutes.
    - Add the minced garlic and cook for an additional minute until fragrant.
3. **Add the Vegetables:**
    - Stir in the diced potatoes, sliced carrots, celery, and bell pepper (if using). Cook for 5 minutes, stirring occasionally.
4. **Add Broth and Seasonings:**
    - Pour in the chicken or vegetable broth and add the diced tomatoes.
    - Stir in the dried thyme, dried oregano, bay leaf, salt, and pepper.
    - Bring the mixture to a boil, then reduce the heat to low and let it simmer for about 15 minutes.
5. **Simmer the Stew:**
    - Add the green beans (if using) and return the cooked sausage to the pot.
    - Continue to simmer for an additional 10-15 minutes, or until the potatoes and vegetables are tender and the sausage is heated through.
6. **Adjust Seasoning:**

- Taste the stew and adjust seasoning with more salt and pepper if needed.
7. **Serve:**
    - Remove the bay leaf before serving.
    - Ladle the stew into bowls and garnish with chopped fresh parsley.

Tips:

- **Sausage Variety:** Choose your favorite sausage or try a mix for added flavor.
- **Vegetable Variations:** Feel free to add other vegetables such as parsnips or turnips based on your preferences.
- **Thickening the Stew:** If you prefer a thicker stew, you can mash some of the potatoes against the side of the pot or stir in a slurry made of 1 tablespoon of flour mixed with 2 tablespoons of water.

Enjoy your Potato and Sausage Stew, a comforting and satisfying dish that's perfect for any time of year!

Baked Sweet Potatoes with Cinnamon

Ingredients:

- 4 medium sweet potatoes
- 2 tablespoons olive oil or melted butter
- 2 tablespoons brown sugar (optional, for extra sweetness)
- 1 teaspoon ground cinnamon
- 1/2 teaspoon ground nutmeg (optional)
- 1/4 teaspoon salt
- Optional toppings: chopped pecans or walnuts, a drizzle of honey or maple syrup

Instructions:

1. **Preheat Oven:**
   - Preheat your oven to 400°F (200°C).
2. **Prepare Sweet Potatoes:**
   - Wash and scrub the sweet potatoes thoroughly. Pat them dry with a paper towel.
   - Pierce each sweet potato several times with a fork to allow steam to escape during baking.
3. **Season the Potatoes:**
   - Rub the sweet potatoes with olive oil or melted butter. This will help the skins become crisp and flavorful.
   - If using brown sugar, mix it with the ground cinnamon, ground nutmeg (if using), and salt in a small bowl.
   - Sprinkle the cinnamon mixture evenly over the sweet potatoes.
4. **Bake:**
   - Place the sweet potatoes on a baking sheet lined with parchment paper or aluminum foil for easy cleanup.
   - Bake in the preheated oven for 45-60 minutes, or until the sweet potatoes are tender and can be easily pierced with a fork. The baking time may vary depending on the size of the sweet potatoes.
5. **Serve:**
   - Once baked, remove the sweet potatoes from the oven and let them cool slightly.
   - If desired, top with chopped pecans or walnuts and a drizzle of honey or maple syrup.

Tips:

- **Sweetness:** If you prefer a less sweet version, you can skip the brown sugar and simply use cinnamon and a pinch of salt.
- **Texture:** For a creamier texture, you can mash the baked sweet potatoes in their skins or scoop out the flesh and mix in additional butter or a splash of milk before serving.
- **Toppings:** Experiment with different toppings such as Greek yogurt, a sprinkle of granola, or a touch of sea salt for added flavor and texture.

Enjoy your Baked Sweet Potatoes with Cinnamon, a warm and comforting side dish that's both easy to prepare and delightful to eat!

Idaho Breakfast Burrito

Ingredients:

- **For the Filling:**
    - 2 large Idaho potatoes, peeled and diced (about 1/2-inch cubes)
    - 1 tablespoon olive oil or butter
    - 1/2 pound breakfast sausage or bacon, cooked and crumbled (or diced, if using bacon)
    - 1/2 cup diced onion
    - 1 bell pepper, diced (any color)
    - 4 large eggs
    - 1/4 cup milk
    - 1 cup shredded cheddar cheese (or your favorite cheese)
    - Salt and freshly ground black pepper, to taste
    - Optional: 1/2 teaspoon paprika or ground cumin for extra flavor
- **For Assembling:**
    - 4 large flour tortillas
    - Optional toppings: salsa, sour cream, avocado, chopped fresh cilantro

Instructions:

1. **Prepare the Potatoes:**
    - Heat olive oil or butter in a large skillet over medium heat.
    - Add the diced potatoes and cook, stirring occasionally, until golden brown and tender, about 15-20 minutes. Season with salt, pepper, and optional paprika or cumin if desired.
    - Remove the cooked potatoes from the skillet and set aside.
2. **Cook the Sausage or Bacon:**
    - In the same skillet, cook the breakfast sausage or bacon until fully cooked and crispy. If using bacon, drain excess fat and crumble or chop the bacon into small pieces.
    - Remove from the skillet and set aside.
3. **Sauté Vegetables:**
    - In the same skillet, add the diced onion and bell pepper. Cook until softened, about 5 minutes.
4. **Scramble the Eggs:**
    - In a bowl, whisk together the eggs and milk. Season with a pinch of salt and pepper.
    - Pour the egg mixture into the skillet with the vegetables and cook, stirring occasionally, until the eggs are fully cooked and scrambled.
5. **Combine Ingredients:**
    - Add the cooked potatoes and sausage (or bacon) back into the skillet with the eggs and vegetables. Stir to combine and heat through.
    - Sprinkle the shredded cheese over the mixture and let it melt.

6. **Assemble the Burritos:**
   - Warm the flour tortillas in a dry skillet or microwave until pliable.
   - Spoon the filling onto the center of each tortilla. Fold the sides over the filling and roll up the burrito from the bottom, tucking in the sides as you go.
7. **Serve:**
   - Optionally, you can toast the assembled burritos in a skillet over medium heat to crisp up the outside.
   - Serve with your choice of optional toppings such as salsa, sour cream, avocado, or chopped fresh cilantro.

Tips:

- **Make Ahead:** You can prepare the filling ahead of time and store it in the refrigerator for up to 3 days. Reheat before assembling the burritos.
- **Vegetable Variations:** Feel free to add other vegetables like mushrooms or spinach to the filling for extra flavor and nutrition.
- **Cheese Choices:** Experiment with different cheeses like Monterey Jack, pepper jack, or feta for varied flavors.

Enjoy your Idaho Breakfast Burrito, a hearty and satisfying meal that's perfect for starting your day on the right foot!

Huckleberry Vinaigrette

Ingredients:

- 1/2 cup fresh or frozen huckleberries (thawed if frozen)
- 1/4 cup red wine vinegar (or balsamic vinegar for a sweeter option)
- 1/4 cup extra-virgin olive oil
- 1 tablespoon honey or maple syrup (adjust based on sweetness preference)
- 1 teaspoon Dijon mustard
- 1 small shallot, finely minced
- 1/4 teaspoon salt
- 1/4 teaspoon freshly ground black pepper
- Optional: 1 teaspoon fresh thyme or rosemary, finely chopped

Instructions:

1. **Prepare the Huckleberries:**
   - If using fresh huckleberries, rinse them under cold water. If using frozen huckleberries, thaw them first and drain any excess liquid.
2. **Make the Vinaigrette:**
   - In a blender or food processor, combine the huckleberries, red wine vinegar, honey (or maple syrup), Dijon mustard, minced shallot, salt, and pepper.
   - Blend until smooth. If the vinaigrette is too thick, you can add a little bit of water to reach your desired consistency.
3. **Add Olive Oil:**
   - With the blender or food processor running on low speed, slowly drizzle in the olive oil until fully incorporated and the vinaigrette is emulsified.
4. **Season and Adjust:**
   - Taste the vinaigrette and adjust the seasoning if necessary. You can add more honey for sweetness, more vinegar for tanginess, or extra salt and pepper to taste.
5. **Optional Herbs:**
   - If using, stir in the chopped fresh thyme or rosemary for additional flavor.
6. **Serve:**
   - Transfer the vinaigrette to a jar or bottle with a tight-fitting lid and refrigerate until ready to use. Shake well before serving.

Tips:

- **Storage:** The vinaigrette can be stored in the refrigerator for up to 1 week. Shake well before each use as the ingredients may separate over time.
- **Usage:** This vinaigrette is excellent on mixed green salads, as a drizzle over roasted vegetables, or as a marinade for grilled chicken or pork.
- **Sweetness:** Adjust the level of sweetness to your taste. You can add more honey or maple syrup if you prefer a sweeter vinaigrette.

Enjoy your Huckleberry Vinaigrette, a delightful and versatile dressing that brings a fresh, fruity twist to your dishes!

Potato and Leek Pie

Ingredients:

- **For the Filling:**
    - 2 tablespoons olive oil or butter
    - 3 large leeks, cleaned and sliced (white and light green parts only)
    - 2 cloves garlic, minced
    - 3 large potatoes, peeled and diced (about 1/2-inch cubes)
    - 1 cup vegetable or chicken broth
    - 1/2 cup heavy cream or whole milk
    - 1 teaspoon dried thyme or fresh thyme leaves
    - Salt and freshly ground black pepper, to taste
    - 1 cup shredded cheese (cheddar, Gruyère, or your choice)
    - Optional: 1 tablespoon chopped fresh parsley for garnish
- **For the Crust:**
    - 1 1/2 cups all-purpose flour
    - 1/2 teaspoon salt
    - 1/2 cup cold butter, cut into small cubes
    - 1/4 cup ice water (more if needed)

Instructions:

1. **Prepare the Crust:**
    - In a medium bowl, combine the flour and salt. Cut in the cold butter using a pastry cutter or your fingers until the mixture resembles coarse crumbs.
    - Gradually add the ice water, a tablespoon at a time, until the dough comes together. You may need slightly more or less water.
    - Form the dough into a disk, wrap in plastic wrap, and refrigerate for at least 30 minutes.
2. **Prepare the Filling:**
    - Heat olive oil or butter in a large skillet over medium heat.
    - Add the sliced leeks and cook, stirring occasionally, until softened, about 5 minutes.
    - Add the minced garlic and cook for an additional minute.
    - Add the diced potatoes and broth. Bring to a boil, then reduce the heat and simmer until the potatoes are tender, about 15-20 minutes.
    - Stir in the heavy cream or milk, thyme, salt, and pepper. Cook for a few more minutes until the mixture thickens slightly. Remove from heat and stir in the shredded cheese.
3. **Assemble the Pie:**
    - Preheat your oven to 375°F (190°C).
    - On a floured surface, roll out the chilled dough to fit a 9-inch pie dish. Transfer the dough to the pie dish, trimming any excess overhang.
    - Pour the potato and leek filling into the prepared pie crust.

- Roll out any remaining dough and place it over the filling, or cut it into strips for a lattice top. Trim and crimp the edges to seal.
- If desired, brush the top crust with a bit of milk or egg wash for a golden finish.

4. **Bake the Pie:**
    - Bake in the preheated oven for 35-40 minutes, or until the crust is golden brown and the filling is bubbly.
    - Let the pie cool for a few minutes before slicing.
5. **Serve:**
    - Garnish with chopped fresh parsley if desired.
    - Serve warm or at room temperature.

Tips:

- **Crust Variations:** For a quicker option, you can use store-bought pie dough or a pre-made pie crust.
- **Flavor Boost:** Add cooked bacon or ham to the filling for extra flavor.
- **Vegetable Variations:** You can include other vegetables such as carrots or peas for added texture and flavor.

Enjoy your Potato and Leek Pie, a comforting and satisfying dish that's perfect for any meal!

Idaho Stuffed Potatoes

Ingredients:

- **For the Potatoes:**
    - 4 large Idaho potatoes
    - 2 tablespoons olive oil
    - Salt and freshly ground black pepper, to taste
- **For the Filling:**
    - 4 strips bacon, cooked and crumbled (optional)
    - 1 cup shredded cheddar cheese
    - 1/2 cup sour cream
    - 1/4 cup milk or heavy cream
    - 1/4 cup chopped green onions or chives
    - 1/2 teaspoon garlic powder
    - 1/4 teaspoon onion powder
    - 1/4 teaspoon paprika
    - Salt and pepper, to taste
    - 1/4 cup chopped fresh parsley (for garnish)

Instructions:

1. **Prepare the Potatoes:**
    - Preheat your oven to 400°F (200°C).
    - Wash and scrub the Idaho potatoes. Pat them dry with a paper towel.
    - Rub the potatoes with olive oil and season with salt and pepper.
    - Place the potatoes on a baking sheet and bake for 45-60 minutes, or until tender when pierced with a fork. Baking time may vary depending on the size of the potatoes.
2. **Prepare the Filling:**
    - While the potatoes are baking, prepare the filling. In a bowl, combine the shredded cheddar cheese, sour cream, milk or heavy cream, chopped green onions, garlic powder, onion powder, paprika, and crumbled bacon (if using). Mix well.
3. **Stuff the Potatoes:**
    - Once the potatoes are baked and cool enough to handle, cut them in half lengthwise.
    - Scoop out the flesh of the potatoes, leaving a small border of potato around the skin. Place the scooped-out flesh in a large bowl.
    - Mash the potato flesh with a fork or potato masher until smooth.
    - Stir the prepared filling into the mashed potatoes. Adjust seasoning with salt and pepper as needed.
4. **Fill and Bake:**
    - Spoon the potato mixture back into the potato skins, mounding it slightly.
    - Return the stuffed potatoes to the baking sheet.

    - Bake in the preheated oven for an additional 15-20 minutes, or until the tops are golden and the filling is heated through.
5. **Serve:**
    - Garnish the stuffed potatoes with chopped fresh parsley before serving.
    - Serve warm as a hearty side dish or a main course.

Tips:

- **Cheese Variations:** Feel free to experiment with different types of cheese, such as Monterey Jack, Gouda, or Parmesan.
- **Add-ins:** Customize the filling by adding ingredients like cooked chicken, sautéed mushrooms, or diced bell peppers.
- **Make Ahead:** You can prepare the stuffed potatoes up to a day in advance. Assemble them, refrigerate, and then bake when ready to serve.

Enjoy your Idaho Stuffed Potatoes, a delicious and versatile dish that's sure to satisfy!

Potato and Bacon Soup

Ingredients:

- **For the Soup:**
    - 6 strips bacon, diced
    - 1 large onion, chopped
    - 3 cloves garlic, minced
    - 4 cups (1 liter) chicken or vegetable broth
    - 4 large potatoes, peeled and diced (about 1/2-inch cubes)
    - 2 cups heavy cream or whole milk
    - 1 teaspoon dried thyme
    - 1/2 teaspoon paprika
    - 1/4 teaspoon ground black pepper
    - 1/2 teaspoon salt (adjust to taste)
    - Optional: 1 cup shredded cheddar cheese
- **For Garnish:**
    - 2 green onions, chopped
    - 1/4 cup chopped fresh parsley
    - Extra crispy bacon bits
    - Optional: Additional shredded cheese

Instructions:

1. **Cook the Bacon:**
    - In a large pot or Dutch oven, cook the diced bacon over medium heat until crispy, about 5-7 minutes.
    - Remove the bacon from the pot with a slotted spoon and place it on a paper towel-lined plate to drain. Leave the bacon drippings in the pot.
2. **Sauté the Vegetables:**
    - Add the chopped onion to the pot with the bacon drippings and cook until softened, about 5 minutes.
    - Add the minced garlic and cook for an additional 1 minute, until fragrant.
3. **Cook the Potatoes:**
    - Add the diced potatoes and chicken or vegetable broth to the pot.
    - Bring the mixture to a boil, then reduce the heat and let it simmer until the potatoes are tender, about 15-20 minutes.
4. **Blend the Soup:**
    - Use an immersion blender to blend the soup until smooth, or transfer the soup in batches to a countertop blender. Be cautious with hot liquids. If you prefer a chunkier texture, blend only half of the soup or mash some of the potatoes with a fork.
5. **Add Cream and Seasonings:**
    - Stir in the heavy cream or milk, dried thyme, paprika, ground black pepper, and salt.

- - Heat the soup over low heat until warmed through. If adding cheese, stir it in at this point and cook until melted.
6. **Serve:**
    - Ladle the soup into bowls and garnish with crispy bacon bits, chopped green onions, fresh parsley, and additional shredded cheese if desired.

Tips:

- **Texture:** For a creamier soup, you can blend all the potatoes. For a chunkier soup, blend only part of the mixture and leave some potato pieces intact.
- **Add-ins:** You can add other vegetables like carrots or celery for extra flavor and nutrition.
- **Storage:** The soup can be stored in the refrigerator for up to 4 days. It also freezes well for up to 3 months. Reheat gently and add a little extra cream or milk if needed.

Enjoy your Potato and Bacon Soup, a rich and satisfying meal that's perfect for warming up on a cold day!

Huckleberry BBQ Ribs

Ingredients:

- **For the Ribs:**
    - 2 racks of baby back ribs (about 2-3 pounds each)
    - 1 tablespoon olive oil
    - 1 tablespoon smoked paprika
    - 1 tablespoon brown sugar
    - 1 tablespoon garlic powder
    - 1 tablespoon onion powder
    - 1 teaspoon ground cumin
    - 1 teaspoon salt
    - 1/2 teaspoon black pepper
    - 1/2 teaspoon chili powder
    - 1/4 teaspoon cayenne pepper (optional, for extra heat)
- **For the Huckleberry BBQ Sauce:**
    - 1 cup fresh or frozen huckleberries (thawed if frozen)
    - 1 cup ketchup
    - 1/4 cup apple cider vinegar
    - 1/4 cup brown sugar
    - 2 tablespoons honey
    - 1 tablespoon Worcestershire sauce
    - 1 teaspoon smoked paprika
    - 1/2 teaspoon garlic powder
    - 1/2 teaspoon onion powder
    - 1/2 teaspoon salt
    - 1/4 teaspoon black pepper

Instructions:

1. **Prepare the Ribs:**
    - Preheat your oven to 300°F (150°C).
    - Remove the membrane from the back of the ribs if it's still attached. This can be done by sliding a knife under the membrane and pulling it off with a paper towel.
    - Rub the ribs with olive oil.
    - In a small bowl, mix together the smoked paprika, brown sugar, garlic powder, onion powder, ground cumin, salt, black pepper, chili powder, and cayenne pepper (if using).
    - Rub the spice mixture evenly over both sides of the ribs.
2. **Bake the Ribs:**
    - Place the ribs on a large piece of aluminum foil, bone side down. Fold the edges of the foil to create a tight seal around the ribs.
    - Place the wrapped ribs on a baking sheet and bake in the preheated oven for 2.5 to 3 hours, until the ribs are tender.

3. **Prepare the Huckleberry BBQ Sauce:**
    - In a medium saucepan, combine the huckleberries, ketchup, apple cider vinegar, brown sugar, honey, Worcestershire sauce, smoked paprika, garlic powder, onion powder, salt, and black pepper.
    - Bring to a simmer over medium heat, stirring occasionally.
    - Cook the sauce for 15-20 minutes, until it has thickened and the huckleberries have broken down. You can use a potato masher to help break up the berries if needed.
    - If you prefer a smoother sauce, blend it with an immersion blender or in a countertop blender.
4. **Grill the Ribs:**
    - Preheat your grill to medium-high heat.
    - Remove the ribs from the oven and discard the foil. Brush a generous amount of huckleberry BBQ sauce over the ribs.
    - Transfer the ribs to the grill and cook for an additional 10-15 minutes, turning occasionally and basting with more BBQ sauce, until the ribs are caramelized and have a nice char.
5. **Serve:**
    - Remove the ribs from the grill and let them rest for a few minutes before slicing between the bones.
    - Serve with extra huckleberry BBQ sauce on the side.

Tips:

- **Marinating:** For extra flavor, you can marinate the ribs in the spice rub overnight in the refrigerator.
- **Cooking Method:** If you prefer, you can cook the ribs entirely on the grill. Just adjust the cooking time and keep an eye on the heat to avoid burning.
- **Huckleberries:** If huckleberries are not available, you can substitute with blueberries or another type of berry for a similar sweet-tart flavor.

Enjoy your Huckleberry BBQ Ribs, a unique and flavorful twist on classic BBQ ribs!

Idaho Potato Frittata

Ingredients:

- **For the Frittata:**
    - 2 tablespoons olive oil or butter
    - 2 large Idaho potatoes, peeled and diced (about 1/2-inch cubes)
    - 1 small onion, finely chopped
    - 1 red bell pepper, diced
    - 1 cup fresh spinach or kale, chopped
    - 6 large eggs
    - 1/2 cup milk or heavy cream
    - 1 cup shredded cheese (cheddar, mozzarella, or your choice)
    - 1 teaspoon dried oregano or thyme
    - Salt and freshly ground black pepper, to taste
    - Optional: 1/2 cup cooked bacon or sausage, crumbled
- **For Garnish (Optional):**
    - Fresh chopped parsley
    - Extra shredded cheese

Instructions:

1. **Cook the Potatoes:**
    - Heat the olive oil or butter in a large ovenproof skillet over medium heat.
    - Add the diced potatoes and cook, stirring occasionally, until they are tender and golden brown, about 10-15 minutes. Remove the potatoes from the skillet and set them aside.
2. **Cook the Vegetables:**
    - In the same skillet, add a little more oil or butter if needed. Add the chopped onion and cook until softened, about 5 minutes.
    - Add the diced bell pepper and cook for an additional 3-4 minutes.
    - Stir in the chopped spinach or kale and cook until wilted. Remove from heat.
3. **Prepare the Egg Mixture:**
    - In a large bowl, whisk together the eggs, milk or heavy cream, shredded cheese, dried oregano or thyme, salt, and pepper.
    - If using bacon or sausage, fold it into the egg mixture.
4. **Combine Ingredients:**
    - Return the cooked potatoes to the skillet with the vegetables.
    - Pour the egg mixture over the potatoes and vegetables, ensuring even distribution.
5. **Cook the Frittata:**
    - Preheat your oven to 375°F (190°C).
    - Cook the frittata on the stovetop over medium heat until the edges begin to set, about 5 minutes.

- Transfer the skillet to the preheated oven and bake for 15-20 minutes, or until the frittata is fully set and the top is lightly golden.
6. **Serve:**
    - Remove the frittata from the oven and let it cool for a few minutes before slicing.
    - Garnish with fresh chopped parsley and extra shredded cheese if desired.

Tips:

- **Customize:** Feel free to add other ingredients like mushrooms, tomatoes, or herbs to suit your taste.
- **Make Ahead:** The frittata can be made ahead and stored in the refrigerator for up to 3 days. It can be served warm or at room temperature.
- **Cooking Vessel:** Make sure to use an ovenproof skillet for this recipe. If you don't have one, you can transfer the mixture to a baking dish before placing it in the oven.

Enjoy your Idaho Potato Frittata, a flavorful and satisfying dish that's perfect for any meal!

Potato and Mushroom Soup

Ingredients:

- **For the Soup:**
    - 2 tablespoons olive oil or butter
    - 1 large onion, chopped
    - 3 cloves garlic, minced
    - 8 ounces (225 grams) mushrooms, sliced (cremini, button, or your choice)
    - 4 large potatoes, peeled and diced (about 1/2-inch cubes)
    - 4 cups (1 liter) vegetable or chicken broth
    - 1 cup heavy cream or whole milk
    - 1 teaspoon dried thyme or fresh thyme leaves
    - 1/2 teaspoon paprika
    - 1/4 teaspoon ground black pepper
    - 1/2 teaspoon salt (adjust to taste)
    - Optional: 1/2 cup white wine or sherry for added depth of flavor
- **For Garnish:**
    - Chopped fresh parsley or chives
    - Extra sautéed mushrooms
    - A drizzle of cream or a sprinkle of grated cheese

Instructions:

1. **Sauté the Vegetables:**
   - Heat the olive oil or butter in a large pot over medium heat.
   - Add the chopped onion and cook until softened, about 5 minutes.
   - Add the minced garlic and cook for an additional minute, until fragrant.
2. **Cook the Mushrooms:**
   - Add the sliced mushrooms to the pot and cook until they release their moisture and become golden brown, about 8-10 minutes.
3. **Add Potatoes and Broth:**
   - Add the diced potatoes to the pot and stir well.
   - Pour in the vegetable or chicken broth. If using white wine or sherry, add it at this point.
   - Bring the mixture to a boil, then reduce the heat and let it simmer until the potatoes are tender, about 15-20 minutes.
4. **Blend the Soup:**
   - Use an immersion blender to blend the soup until smooth, or transfer the soup in batches to a countertop blender. Be cautious with hot liquids. If you prefer a chunkier texture, blend only half of the soup or mash some of the potatoes with a fork.
5. **Add Cream and Seasonings:**
   - Stir in the heavy cream or milk, dried thyme, paprika, ground black pepper, and salt.

        ○ Heat the soup over low heat until warmed through. Adjust seasoning as needed.
    6. **Serve:**
        ○ Ladle the soup into bowls and garnish with chopped fresh parsley or chives, extra sautéed mushrooms, and a drizzle of cream or a sprinkle of cheese if desired.

Tips:

- **Mushroom Variety:** Feel free to use a mix of mushrooms for a richer flavor.
- **Texture:** For a smoother soup, you can blend it completely, or for a heartier texture, blend only half and leave some potato and mushroom pieces whole.
- **Make Ahead:** The soup can be made ahead and stored in the refrigerator for up to 4 days. It also freezes well for up to 3 months. Reheat gently and adjust seasoning as needed.

Enjoy your Potato and Mushroom Soup, a warm and satisfying dish that's perfect for any meal!

Huckleberry Oatmeal Cookies

Ingredients:

- **For the Cookies:**
    - 1 cup (2 sticks) unsalted butter, softened
    - 1 cup granulated sugar
    - 1 cup packed brown sugar
    - 2 large eggs
    - 1 teaspoon vanilla extract
    - 1 1/2 cups all-purpose flour
    - 1 teaspoon baking soda
    - 1/2 teaspoon baking powder
    - 1/2 teaspoon salt
    - 3 cups old-fashioned rolled oats
    - 1 cup fresh or frozen huckleberries (thawed if frozen)
- **For Optional Add-ins:**
    - 1/2 cup chopped nuts (e.g., walnuts, pecans)
    - 1/2 cup white or dark chocolate chips

Instructions:

1. **Preheat the Oven:**
    - Preheat your oven to 350°F (175°C).
    - Line baking sheets with parchment paper or silicone baking mats.
2. **Prepare the Dough:**
    - In a large bowl, cream together the softened butter, granulated sugar, and brown sugar until light and fluffy.
    - Beat in the eggs one at a time, then stir in the vanilla extract.
3. **Mix Dry Ingredients:**
    - In a separate bowl, whisk together the flour, baking soda, baking powder, and salt.
4. **Combine Ingredients:**
    - Gradually add the dry ingredients to the butter mixture, mixing until just combined.
    - Stir in the oats until evenly distributed.
    - Gently fold in the huckleberries and optional add-ins like nuts or chocolate chips if using.
5. **Form the Cookies:**
    - Drop rounded tablespoons of dough onto the prepared baking sheets, spacing them about 2 inches apart.
6. **Bake the Cookies:**
    - Bake in the preheated oven for 12-15 minutes, or until the edges are golden brown but the centers are still soft.
    - Remove from the oven and let the cookies cool on the baking sheets for a few minutes before transferring them to a wire rack to cool completely.
7. **Serve:**

- Enjoy the cookies once they have cooled, or store them in an airtight container for up to a week.

Tips:

- **Huckleberries:** If fresh huckleberries are not available, you can use frozen ones. Just be sure to thaw and drain them to avoid excess moisture in the dough.
- **Consistency:** If the dough seems too soft, you can chill it in the refrigerator for about 30 minutes before baking.
- **Variations:** Feel free to customize these cookies by adding your favorite mix-ins like dried fruits, other berries, or spices.

Enjoy your Huckleberry Oatmeal Cookies, a sweet and chewy treat that combines the best flavors of summer with classic oatmeal cookie goodness!

Idaho Roasted Potatoes with Herbs

Ingredients:

- **For the Potatoes:**
    - 2 pounds Idaho potatoes (Yukon Gold or Russet work well), peeled and cut into 1-inch cubes
    - 3 tablespoons olive oil
    - 1 tablespoon fresh rosemary, chopped (or 1 teaspoon dried rosemary)
    - 1 tablespoon fresh thyme, chopped (or 1 teaspoon dried thyme)
    - 4 cloves garlic, minced
    - 1 teaspoon paprika
    - 1/2 teaspoon onion powder
    - 1/2 teaspoon garlic powder
    - 1/2 teaspoon salt (adjust to taste)
    - 1/4 teaspoon black pepper (adjust to taste)
    - Optional: 1 tablespoon fresh parsley, chopped for garnish

Instructions:

1. **Preheat the Oven:**
    - Preheat your oven to 425°F (220°C).
    - Line a baking sheet with parchment paper or lightly grease it with cooking spray.
2. **Prepare the Potatoes:**
    - Place the cubed potatoes in a large mixing bowl.
    - Drizzle the olive oil over the potatoes and toss to coat evenly.
3. **Season the Potatoes:**
    - In a small bowl, mix together the rosemary, thyme, minced garlic, paprika, onion powder, garlic powder, salt, and black pepper.
    - Sprinkle the seasoning mixture over the potatoes and toss until all the pieces are well-coated with the herbs and spices.
4. **Roast the Potatoes:**
    - Spread the seasoned potatoes in a single layer on the prepared baking sheet.
    - Roast in the preheated oven for 25-30 minutes, or until the potatoes are golden brown and crispy on the outside, and tender on the inside. Be sure to toss the potatoes halfway through the roasting time for even cooking.
5. **Garnish and Serve:**
    - Remove the potatoes from the oven and, if desired, sprinkle with fresh chopped parsley.
    - Serve the roasted potatoes hot as a side dish with your favorite main course.

Tips:

- **Cut Uniformly:** Cut the potatoes into evenly sized cubes to ensure they cook evenly.
- **Crispier Potatoes:** For extra crispiness, you can preheat the baking sheet in the oven before adding the potatoes.

- **Make Ahead:** You can prepare the potatoes ahead of time and toss them with the olive oil and seasonings. Store them in the refrigerator until ready to roast.

Enjoy your Idaho Roasted Potatoes with Herbs, a simple yet delicious side dish that pairs well with a variety of main courses!

Potato and Kale Salad

Ingredients:

- **For the Salad:**
    - 1 1/2 pounds baby potatoes or Yukon Gold potatoes, scrubbed and halved
    - 4 cups kale, stems removed and leaves chopped
    - 1/4 cup red onion, thinly sliced
    - 1/2 cup cherry tomatoes, halved
    - 1/4 cup feta cheese, crumbled (optional)
    - 1/4 cup sliced black olives (optional)
- **For the Dressing:**
    - 1/4 cup extra-virgin olive oil
    - 2 tablespoons red wine vinegar or lemon juice
    - 1 teaspoon Dijon mustard
    - 1 clove garlic, minced
    - 1 teaspoon honey or maple syrup
    - Salt and freshly ground black pepper, to taste

Instructions:

1. **Cook the Potatoes:**
    - Bring a large pot of salted water to a boil.
    - Add the halved potatoes and cook until tender, about 10-15 minutes. You can check for doneness by poking a potato with a fork; it should easily go through.
    - Drain the potatoes and let them cool slightly.
2. **Prepare the Kale:**
    - While the potatoes are cooking, place the chopped kale in a large bowl.
    - Massage the kale with a bit of olive oil and a pinch of salt for a couple of minutes until the kale becomes slightly tender and darkens in color.
3. **Prepare the Dressing:**
    - In a small bowl or jar, whisk together the olive oil, red wine vinegar or lemon juice, Dijon mustard, minced garlic, honey or maple syrup, salt, and black pepper until well combined.
4. **Assemble the Salad:**
    - Add the slightly cooled potatoes, red onion, and cherry tomatoes to the bowl with the kale.
    - Pour the dressing over the salad and gently toss to combine, ensuring that all ingredients are well-coated with the dressing.
    - If using feta cheese and black olives, sprinkle them over the top and give the salad a final toss.
5. **Serve:**
    - The salad can be served immediately or allowed to sit for 30 minutes to let the flavors meld together. It can be served warm, at room temperature, or chilled.

Tips:

- **Add Protein:** For a more filling salad, consider adding grilled chicken, chickpeas, or hard-boiled eggs.
- **Customize:** Feel free to add other vegetables or ingredients like bell peppers, cucumbers, or avocado to suit your taste.
- **Make Ahead:** The salad can be made ahead of time and stored in the refrigerator for up to 3 days. If the kale seems to have wilted too much, just give it a good toss before serving.

Enjoy your Potato and Kale Salad, a nutritious and delicious option that pairs well with a variety of meals!

Huckleberry Tart

Ingredients:

- **For the Tart Crust:**
    - 1 1/2 cups all-purpose flour
    - 1/4 cup granulated sugar
    - 1/2 teaspoon salt
    - 1/2 cup (1 stick) unsalted butter, cold and cut into small pieces
    - 1 large egg yolk
    - 1-2 tablespoons cold water (as needed)
- **For the Huckleberry Filling:**
    - 2 cups fresh or frozen huckleberries (thawed and drained if frozen)
    - 1/2 cup granulated sugar
    - 2 tablespoons cornstarch
    - 1 tablespoon lemon juice
    - 1 teaspoon lemon zest
    - 1/4 teaspoon salt
- **For the Topping:**
    - 1 tablespoon granulated sugar (for sprinkling on top)
    - Optional: Whipped cream or vanilla ice cream for serving

Instructions:

1. **Prepare the Tart Crust:**
    - Preheat your oven to 375°F (190°C).
    - In a food processor, combine the flour, sugar, and salt. Pulse to mix.
    - Add the cold butter and pulse until the mixture resembles coarse crumbs.
    - Add the egg yolk and pulse until combined. Gradually add cold water, 1 tablespoon at a time, until the dough comes together.
    - Transfer the dough to a lightly floured surface and gently knead until smooth. Roll out the dough to fit a 9-inch tart pan with a removable bottom.
    - Press the dough into the tart pan, trimming any excess. Prick the bottom of the crust with a fork.
2. **Blind Bake the Crust:**
    - Place a piece of parchment paper over the crust and fill with pie weights or dried beans.
    - Bake in the preheated oven for 15 minutes.
    - Remove the parchment and weights and bake for an additional 5-7 minutes, or until the crust is golden brown. Allow to cool.
3. **Prepare the Huckleberry Filling:**
    - In a medium saucepan, combine the huckleberries, sugar, cornstarch, lemon juice, lemon zest, and salt.
    - Cook over medium heat, stirring constantly, until the mixture begins to thicken and bubble, about 5-7 minutes.
    - Remove from heat and let cool slightly.
4. **Assemble the Tart:**
    - Pour the huckleberry filling into the cooled tart crust, spreading it evenly.
5. **Bake the Tart:**

- Sprinkle the top of the tart with granulated sugar.
- Bake in the preheated oven for 10-15 minutes, or until the filling is bubbly and the edges of the tart are golden.

6. **Cool and Serve:**
    - Allow the tart to cool completely before removing it from the pan.
    - Serve with whipped cream or vanilla ice cream if desired.

Tips:

- **Crust Variations:** You can also use a pre-made tart shell or a graham cracker crust if you prefer a different base.
- **Filling Variations:** If huckleberries are not available, you can substitute with blueberries, raspberries, or blackberries.
- **Storage:** The tart can be stored in the refrigerator for up to 3 days. It can also be frozen for up to 2 months. Thaw before serving.

Enjoy your Huckleberry Tart, a delicious and elegant dessert that showcases the unique flavor of huckleberries!

Idaho Beef and Potato Stew

Ingredients:

- **For the Stew:**
    - 2 pounds beef chuck, cut into 1-inch cubes
    - 2 tablespoons vegetable oil
    - 1 large onion, chopped
    - 3 cloves garlic, minced
    - 4 cups beef broth
    - 1 cup red wine (optional, can substitute with additional beef broth)
    - 4 large Idaho potatoes, peeled and cut into 1-inch cubes
    - 3 carrots, peeled and sliced into 1/2-inch pieces
    - 2 celery stalks, sliced
    - 1 cup frozen peas (or fresh if in season)
    - 2 tablespoons tomato paste
    - 1 teaspoon dried thyme
    - 1 teaspoon dried rosemary
    - 1 bay leaf
    - 1/4 cup all-purpose flour
    - Salt and freshly ground black pepper, to taste
- **For Garnish (optional):**
    - Fresh chopped parsley

Instructions:

1. **Brown the Beef:**
    - In a large pot or Dutch oven, heat the vegetable oil over medium-high heat.
    - Add the beef cubes in batches (do not overcrowd) and brown on all sides. Remove the beef and set aside.
2. **Sauté the Aromatics:**
    - In the same pot, add the chopped onion and cook until softened, about 5 minutes.
    - Add the minced garlic and cook for an additional 1 minute, until fragrant.
3. **Deglaze the Pot:**
    - If using, pour in the red wine and scrape up any browned bits from the bottom of the pot.
    - Allow the wine to reduce slightly for about 2 minutes.
4. **Combine Ingredients:**
    - Return the browned beef to the pot.
    - Stir in the tomato paste and cook for 2 minutes.
    - Sprinkle the flour over the beef and vegetables, stirring well to coat.
5. **Add Liquids and Seasonings:**
    - Pour in the beef broth and stir to combine.
    - Add the dried thyme, dried rosemary, bay leaf, salt, and black pepper.
    - Bring the mixture to a boil, then reduce the heat to low and cover.
6. **Simmer the Stew:**
    - Simmer the stew for 1.5 to 2 hours, or until the beef is tender and the flavors have melded together.

7. **Add Vegetables:**
   - Add the potatoes, carrots, and celery to the pot.
   - Continue to simmer for an additional 30-40 minutes, or until the vegetables are tender.
8. **Finish and Serve:**
   - Stir in the frozen peas and cook for an additional 5 minutes.
   - Adjust seasoning with salt and pepper as needed.
   - Remove the bay leaf before serving.
   - Garnish with fresh chopped parsley if desired.

Tips:

- **Beef Selection:** Choose a well-marbled cut of beef, like chuck, for tender results. If you prefer, you can use pre-cut stew meat.
- **Thickening:** If the stew needs to be thicker, you can mix a tablespoon of cornstarch with a little cold water and stir it into the stew. Cook for an additional 5 minutes until thickened.
- **Flavor Boost:** Adding a splash of balsamic vinegar or a teaspoon of Worcestershire sauce can enhance the flavor.

Enjoy your Idaho Beef and Potato Stew, a comforting and satisfying dish that's perfect for any occasion!

Potato and Cheddar Soup

Ingredients:

- **For the Soup:**
    - 4 tablespoons unsalted butter
    - 1 large onion, chopped
    - 2 cloves garlic, minced
    - 4 cups peeled and diced potatoes (about 4 medium-sized potatoes)
    - 4 cups chicken or vegetable broth
    - 1 cup milk
    - 1 cup heavy cream
    - 2 cups shredded sharp cheddar cheese
    - 1 teaspoon dried thyme
    - 1/2 teaspoon paprika
    - Salt and freshly ground black pepper, to taste
- **For Garnish (optional):**
    - 1/4 cup chopped fresh chives or green onions
    - Extra shredded cheddar cheese
    - Crumbled bacon
    - Sour cream

Instructions:

1. **Sauté the Aromatics:**
    - In a large pot, melt the butter over medium heat.
    - Add the chopped onion and cook until softened and translucent, about 5 minutes.
    - Add the minced garlic and cook for an additional 1 minute until fragrant.
2. **Cook the Potatoes:**
    - Add the diced potatoes to the pot and stir to combine with the onions and garlic.
    - Pour in the chicken or vegetable broth and bring to a boil.
    - Reduce the heat to low and simmer until the potatoes are tender, about 15-20 minutes.
3. **Blend the Soup:**
    - Using an immersion blender, blend the soup directly in the pot until smooth. Alternatively, you can transfer the soup in batches to a blender and blend until smooth. Be careful with the hot liquid!
4. **Add Dairy and Cheese:**
    - Return the blended soup to the pot (if you used a blender).
    - Stir in the milk and heavy cream. Heat the soup over medium heat until warmed through.
    - Add the shredded cheddar cheese a little at a time, stirring until fully melted and the soup is creamy.
5. **Season the Soup:**
    - Stir in the dried thyme and paprika.
    - Season with salt and black pepper to taste.
6. **Serve:**

- Ladle the soup into bowls and garnish with your choice of chopped chives or green onions, extra shredded cheddar cheese, crumbled bacon, and/or a dollop of sour cream.

Tips:

- **Potatoes:** Use starchy potatoes like Russet for a creamy texture. If you prefer a chunkier soup, reserve some of the potato chunks before blending and stir them back in after blending.
- **Cheese:** For a sharper flavor, use aged cheddar. You can also experiment with other cheeses like Gruyère or Gouda.
- **Thickening:** If you prefer a thicker soup, you can use a potato masher to mash some of the potatoes instead of blending the entire batch.

Enjoy your Potato and Cheddar Soup, a rich and comforting dish that's perfect for a cozy meal!

Huckleberry Pancake Syrup

Ingredients:

- 2 cups fresh or frozen huckleberries (thawed if frozen)
- 1 cup granulated sugar
- 1/2 cup water
- 1 tablespoon lemon juice
- 1 teaspoon lemon zest
- 1/2 teaspoon vanilla extract
- 1/4 teaspoon ground cinnamon (optional)
- 1/4 teaspoon salt

Instructions:

1. **Combine Ingredients:**
   - In a medium saucepan, combine the huckleberries, granulated sugar, and water.
   - Bring the mixture to a boil over medium-high heat, stirring occasionally.
2. **Simmer the Syrup:**
   - Reduce the heat to low and let the mixture simmer for 10-15 minutes, or until the berries have softened and the syrup has thickened slightly. Stir occasionally.
3. **Blend (Optional):**
   - For a smoother syrup, use an immersion blender to blend the mixture directly in the saucepan until smooth. Alternatively, you can transfer the mixture to a blender and blend in batches, then return to the saucepan.
4. **Add Flavorings:**
   - Stir in the lemon juice, lemon zest, vanilla extract, and ground cinnamon (if using).
   - Continue to simmer for another 2-3 minutes to let the flavors meld together.
5. **Strain (Optional):**
   - If you prefer a clear syrup, strain the mixture through a fine-mesh sieve to remove the berry seeds and pulp. Press down with a spoon to extract as much liquid as possible.
6. **Cool and Store:**
   - Allow the syrup to cool slightly before transferring it to a clean jar or bottle.
   - Store the syrup in the refrigerator for up to 2 weeks.
7. **Serve:**
   - Heat the syrup slightly before serving if it has thickened too much in the refrigerator.

Tips:

- **Sweetness Level:** Adjust the sugar amount to taste if you prefer a sweeter or less sweet syrup.
- **Consistency:** If the syrup becomes too thick after cooling, you can thin it with a bit of water or additional lemon juice.

- **Berry Substitutes:** If huckleberries are not available, you can use blueberries or raspberries as an alternative, though the flavor will be slightly different.

Enjoy your Huckleberry Pancake Syrup, a deliciously fruity topping for your breakfast favorites!

Idaho Chicken Pot Pie

Ingredients:

- **For the Filling:**
    - 1 tablespoon vegetable oil
    - 1 pound boneless, skinless chicken breasts or thighs, diced
    - 1 medium onion, chopped
    - 2 cloves garlic, minced
    - 2 cups Idaho potatoes, peeled and diced
    - 1 cup carrots, peeled and diced
    - 1 cup celery, diced
    - 1 cup frozen peas
    - 1/2 cup all-purpose flour
    - 1 cup chicken broth
    - 1 cup milk
    - 1 cup shredded cheddar cheese (optional)
    - 1 teaspoon dried thyme
    - 1 teaspoon dried rosemary
    - Salt and freshly ground black pepper, to taste
- **For the Pie Crust:**
    - 1 package refrigerated pie crusts (or homemade if preferred)
    - 1 egg, beaten (for egg wash)

Instructions:

1. **Prepare the Filling:**
    - Preheat your oven to 400°F (200°C).
    - Heat the vegetable oil in a large skillet or saucepan over medium heat.
    - Add the diced chicken and cook until browned and cooked through, about 5-7 minutes. Remove the chicken from the skillet and set aside.
    - In the same skillet, add the chopped onion, garlic, diced potatoes, carrots, and celery. Cook until the vegetables begin to soften, about 5-7 minutes.
    - Stir in the flour and cook for another 2 minutes, allowing the flour to coat the vegetables and absorb any liquid.
    - Gradually add the chicken broth and milk, stirring constantly until the mixture thickens and becomes creamy.
    - Return the cooked chicken to the skillet. Stir in the frozen peas, cheddar cheese (if using), dried thyme, dried rosemary, salt, and black pepper.
    - Cook for an additional 5 minutes, until the filling is thick and well combined.
2. **Assemble the Pie:**
    - Roll out one pie crust and fit it into a 9-inch pie dish.
    - Pour the chicken filling into the pie crust, spreading it evenly.
    - Roll out the second pie crust and place it over the filling. Trim any excess crust and crimp the edges to seal.
    - Cut a few slits in the top crust to allow steam to escape. Brush the top crust with the beaten egg for a golden finish.

3. **Bake the Pie:**
   - Place the pie on a baking sheet to catch any drips.
   - Bake in the preheated oven for 35-45 minutes, or until the crust is golden brown and the filling is bubbling.
4. **Cool and Serve:**
   - Allow the pot pie to cool for about 10 minutes before serving. This helps the filling set and makes it easier to cut.

Tips:

- **Crust:** If you prefer a homemade pie crust, you can use your favorite recipe or use pre-made crusts for convenience.
- **Vegetables:** Feel free to add other vegetables like corn or green beans to the filling.
- **Make Ahead:** The filling can be prepared a day in advance and stored in the refrigerator. Assemble and bake the pie on the day you plan to serve it.

Enjoy your Idaho Chicken Pot Pie, a classic comfort dish that's sure to please!

Sweet Potato and Black Bean Chili

Ingredients:

- **For the Chili:**
    - 1 tablespoon olive oil
    - 1 medium onion, chopped
    - 2 cloves garlic, minced
    - 1 bell pepper (any color), chopped
    - 2 medium sweet potatoes, peeled and diced
    - 1 cup carrots, peeled and diced
    - 2 cans (15 oz each) black beans, drained and rinsed
    - 1 can (15 oz) diced tomatoes
    - 1 can (15 oz) tomato sauce
    - 1 cup vegetable broth (or chicken broth)
    - 2 tablespoons chili powder
    - 1 teaspoon ground cumin
    - 1/2 teaspoon smoked paprika
    - 1/4 teaspoon cayenne pepper (optional, for heat)
    - 1 teaspoon dried oregano
    - 1 teaspoon dried thyme
    - Salt and freshly ground black pepper, to taste
- **For Garnish (optional):**
    - Fresh chopped cilantro
    - Sliced green onions
    - Shredded cheddar cheese
    - Sour cream
    - Sliced jalapeños

Instructions:

1. **Sauté the Aromatics:**
    - Heat the olive oil in a large pot or Dutch oven over medium heat.
    - Add the chopped onion and cook until softened, about 5 minutes.
    - Add the minced garlic and chopped bell pepper, and cook for an additional 2 minutes.
2. **Cook the Vegetables:**
    - Stir in the diced sweet potatoes and carrots. Cook for about 5 minutes, allowing the vegetables to begin to soften.
3. **Add Beans and Tomatoes:**
    - Add the black beans, diced tomatoes, tomato sauce, and vegetable broth to the pot.
    - Stir in the chili powder, ground cumin, smoked paprika, cayenne pepper (if using), dried oregano, and dried thyme.
4. **Simmer the Chili:**
    - Bring the mixture to a boil.

- Reduce the heat to low, cover, and let it simmer for about 25-30 minutes, or until the sweet potatoes and carrots are tender.
5. **Season and Adjust:**
   - Taste the chili and adjust the seasoning with salt and black pepper as needed.
6. **Serve:**
   - Ladle the chili into bowls and garnish with your choice of cilantro, green onions, shredded cheddar cheese, sour cream, and/or sliced jalapeños.

Tips:

- **Vegetable Variations:** Feel free to add other vegetables like corn, zucchini, or bell peppers to the chili.
- **Spice Level:** Adjust the amount of cayenne pepper or chili powder based on your heat preference.
- **Make Ahead:** The chili can be made in advance and stored in the refrigerator for up to 4 days. It also freezes well for up to 3 months.

Enjoy your Sweet Potato and Black Bean Chili, a nutritious and delicious option for any meal!

Huckleberry Smoothie Bowl

Ingredients:

- **For the Smoothie Base:**
    - 1 cup fresh or frozen huckleberries (thawed if frozen)
    - 1 banana, sliced (fresh or frozen)
    - 1/2 cup plain or vanilla Greek yogurt
    - 1/2 cup almond milk (or any milk of your choice)
    - 1 tablespoon honey or maple syrup (optional, adjust to taste)
    - 1 tablespoon chia seeds or flaxseeds (optional, for added nutrition)
- **For Toppings:**
    - Fresh huckleberries or other berries
    - Sliced banana
    - Granola
    - Chia seeds or flaxseeds
    - Nuts (e.g., almonds, walnuts)
    - Coconut flakes
    - A drizzle of honey or maple syrup

Instructions:

1. **Prepare the Smoothie Base:**
    - In a blender, combine the huckleberries, banana, Greek yogurt, almond milk, and honey (if using).
    - Blend until smooth. If the mixture is too thick, add a little more almond milk to reach your desired consistency.
2. **Assemble the Smoothie Bowl:**
    - Pour the smoothie into a bowl.
    - Arrange your desired toppings on the surface of the smoothie in an appealing pattern.
3. **Serve:**
    - Enjoy immediately for the best texture and flavor.

Tips:

- **Consistency:** If you prefer a thicker smoothie bowl, use less liquid or add more frozen fruit.
- **Toppings:** Feel free to customize your toppings based on what you have on hand or your preferences. Fresh fruit, nuts, seeds, and granola add a great crunch and extra nutrients.
- **Sweetness:** Adjust the sweetness of the smoothie base by adding more honey or maple syrup if needed.

This Huckleberry Smoothie Bowl is a delicious and healthy way to start your day or enjoy as a refreshing snack!